2.60.

ARCHERY

About the authors

Dr. Wayne C. McKinney is a Professor, and Head of the Health and Physical Education Department at Southwest Missouri State University in Springfield, Missouri. He earned A.B. and A.M. degrees with honors at California State University at Long Beach, and he earned the Ph.D. at The University of Southern California. As an undergraduate student-athlete, Dr. McKinney participated in intercollegiate athletics, football and baseball, at CSULB.

As an author or coauthor, Dr. McKinney has had articles published in the following journals: *National College Physical Education Association Proceedings, Quest, Journal of Health, Physical Education and Recreation, Missouri Journal of Health, Physical Education and Recreation, Scholastic Coach, Athletic Journal, The Journal of the Association for Physical and Mental Rehabilitation, The Physical Educator, Southwest Missourian,* and *Track and Field Guide.*

Dr. McKinney has authored three editions of *Archery* for WCB. He has also coauthored the following books published by WCB: *Biophysical Values of Muscular Activity* (second edition), *Kinesiology,* and *Introduction to Biomechanic Analysis of Sport.*

Dr. McKinney is also a member of The Research Council of The American Alliance of Health, Physical Education and Recreation.

ARCHERY

Physical Education Activities Series

Wayne C. McKinney
Southwest Missouri State University

THIRD EDITION

Wm C Brown Company Publishers
Dubuque, Iowa

CONSULTING EDITOR

Aileene Lockhart
Texas Woman's University

EVALUATION MATERIALS EDITOR

Jane Mott
Smith College

Copyright © 1966, 1971, 1975 by Wm. C. Brown Company Publishers

Library of Congress Catalog Card Number: 74-27901

ISBN 0—697—07059—X

Printed in the United States of America

Contents

Preface

This book was written for the beginning archer. Specifically, it was designed for college or university students interested in learning the skills of archery and the various ways in which archery may be utilized avocationally throughout their lifetimes. These ways include target archery, bow hunting, bow fishing, and field archery. In addition, the book briefly introduces the reader to archery as it relates to some fascinating aspects of history, literature, art, and science. Development of archery skill combined with an understanding of the academic aspects of archery contribute to the university student's liberal arts education in a meaningful way, and both have the potential for enhancing one's leisure time.

Acknowledgment is made to Doug Kittredge of Mammoth, California. Our informal discussions about archery several years ago at the University of Southern California led indirectly to the writing of this book. I also appreciate the fact that Dr. Aileene Lockhart asked me to write it.

Appreciation is extended to Wilson Brothers, of Springfield, Missouri, manufacturers of Black Widow bows. Their help and advice about archery tackle over the years is appreciated. Dr. L. Dennis Humphrey's photographic work is appreciated. Acknowledgment is also made to Mike McKinney for his assistance as the archer who modeled for most of the illustrations.

Special acknowledgment is made to E. G. Heath of England for granting permission to reproduce several illustrations from *The Grey Goose Wing*, his classic book on the subject of archery published by Osprey Publishing Limited in Berkshire, England.

Finally, the work of Rita Needham in typing and preparing the manuscript is appreciated.

The content and purpose of the book, together with possible errors, are the sole responsibility of the author.

WAYNE C. McKINNEY

Archery tackle

1

"Archery tackle" is the term used by archers for their equipment. There is an axiom that an athlete will be as good or poor as his or her equipment, and it is very true as regards archery. Consequently, tackle should be one of the first things considered by a person interested in learning this sport.

The beginner should be provided with every opportunity to learn the sport efficiently. This requires that archery tackle be *matched*, i.e., arrows, exactly alike in every detail, should be matched for use with a specific bow suitable for the individual archer. Each archer differs in regard to strength, length of limbs, and aesthetic preferences. Therefore tackle, whether issued by universities or purchased by individuals should suit the specific anatomic requirements and other factors of difference of each individual archer.

A beginner who is mismatched for archery tackle will experience considerable frustration. For example, it is actually possible to perform all fundamentals correctly with inferior tackle, yet have little success as far as accuracy is concerned. In target archery, it is absolutely essential that the archer obtain a consistent, tight grouping pattern on the target. With cheap or mismatched tackle each arrow shot will have a different flight pattern, resulting in very erratic arrow grouping. Overcoming the human factors that contribute to mistakes and accuracy is enough in and of itself to make archery a challenging sport for beginner and expert alike. The archer should not be burdened with the use of inefficient tackle which would only add to the unique problems and challenges inherent in learning to become accurate in target archery, field archery, bow-hunting, or bow-fishing situations.

The beginning archer should start shooting with tackle issued by a qualified archery instructor. Cost of tackle can be prohibitive for the university student. Due to this economic factor, the student should try the sport for a period of time to determine whether or not it appeals to his or her recreational interests. If archery becomes an interest as a lifetime sport, it is recommended that tackle then be purchased from a professional archery shop. Sporting goods, hardware, and department stores are usually poor places to purchase tackle unless their salesmen are completely cognizant of the technical and scientific aspects of archery tackle.

It is recommended that the archer who plans to use archery as an avocational activity purchase the following units of tackle as a minimum: (1) twelve fiberglass or aluminum arrows with target points; (2) a working recurve or takedown bow with center shot design; (3) one leather finger tab; (4) one leather arm guard; (5) one arrow quiver; (6) a bowstringer; and (7) a finger or bow sling. This minimum amount of matched tackle is enough to enable the archer to learn archery efficiently. The overall cost depends upon the quality of tackle purchased. One basic principle to keep in mind in regard to the economic factor is this: Cost should never be reduced by purchasing inexpensive arrows. The arrow is the most important single item of tackle. Cost can be reduced by purchasing a used bow and cheaper accessories during the learning period.

THE ARROW

Although wooden arrows are available on the market, only fiberglass and aluminum arrows are recommended.

Fiberglass arrows are satisfactory for use by learners. They are manufactured with precision. During the past decade, research has led to the development of a light, durable, and hollow fiberglass shaft—highly acceptable for quality arrows. It is possible for arrow manufacturers to maintain quality control to the point that there are only microscopic deviations in regard to shaft thickness, shaft diameter, and actual arrow weight. The fiberglass arrow shaft always remains straight. This is a distinct advantage of the fiberglass arrow over the aluminum arrow shaft. The fiberglass, like the wooden arrow, will break if it strikes a target stand or other hard object at an odd angle. The frequency with which this occurs is minimal. Fiberglass arrows can, however, be smashed if stepped on, because the shafts are hollow.

Aluminum arrows are the finest and most accurate on the market today. Aluminum alloys allow manufacturers to construct arrows which are nearly perfect. When shot by a machine during testing from fifty yards, it is not uncommon to see arrows grouped within a diameter of two inches. Aluminum arrows are, however, the most expensive on the market. If the beginner desires to purchase aluminum arrows initially, he should bear in mind that there will be times when these arrows will completely miss the target and become lost in the grass. Also, aluminum shafts, unlike fiberglass arrows, will bend when they strike the target stand or other hard objects instead of the target mat. (There are, however, procedures for straightening a bent aluminum shaft.) If the beginner will accept these factors prior to purchasing, he will choose aluminum arrows, which are highly recommended as compared to fiberglass arrows. James D. Easton, Incorporated, in Van Nuys, California, produce some of the best aluminum shafts in the world.

The novice who uses a matched end of arrows—six arrows with the same physical weight, degree of shaft stiffness (spine), length, and fletching (feathers)—will shoot more accurately than the beginning archer who shoots unmatched arrows. Terminology for the various parts of the arrow is shown in figure 1.1. Figure 1.2 shows four common types of arrows used in target archery, bow hunting, field archery, and bow fishing. The reader should visually compare and contrast the various parts of these arrows keeping in mind that they were designed for entirely different purposes.

Spine

The spine of an arrow shaft is the deflection of the shaft, measured in inches, when depressed by a two-pound weight at its center. There are instruments which measure the degree of spine with minute precision. This

Fig. 1.1.   Arrow terminology.

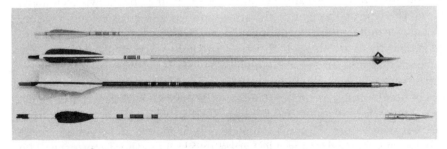

Fig. 1.2.   Arrow designs. From top to bottom: Target, bow hunting, field, and bow fishing.

measurement is important, inasmuch as the degree of spine is a basic factor to consider when obtaining arrows. Spine must be compatible with the archer's bow weight. One reason for matching bow weight and spine is a phenomenon known as the *Archer's Paradox*. Contrary to what the archer thinks he sees as the arrow leaves the bow, an arrow does not fly straight toward the target immediately upon being released. By means of cinematographic analysis, it has been clearly demonstrated that the arrow shaft actually deflects around the bow immediately after release. The reader can readily understand that an arrow shaft too stiff or flexible could cause problems during this phase of its flight pattern. An arrow of sufficient spine, *which has been released properly*, tends to stabilize itself rapidly and follows a straight flight pattern during its trajectory toward the target. The fact that an arrow first deviates to the left for a right-handed archer when it leaves the bow, but stabilizes itself in flight to travel directly to the intended target, is known as the *Archer's Paradox*.

What are some of the consequences of having improperly spined arrows for a bow? (It must be kept in mind that several factors other than spine are also involved with accurate arrow flight. These will be discussed later.) Improper spine can cause the following arrow flight patterns: (1) an arrow naturally starts its flight by deviating a few degrees to the left for a right-handed archer. If the spine is too stiff, the shaft of the arrow or the fletching will actually brush the bow. This causes a reduction in arrow velocity. In addition, a flight pattern change occurs in the opposite direction. The archer's shot will be low and to the right of the intended target, or (2) if the spine is too weak and flexible, the arrow may never stabilize and follow its intended trajectory. Instead, it will fly consistently to the left of the target. Improperly spined arrows are a definite causative factor for erratic arrow grouping.

What should be considered when selecting the proper spine for arrows? First, *the bow weight, i.e., the pounds of pull exerted on the bowstring by the archer for his or her specific arrow length*, is very important. Second, the arrow length and weight to the grain must be known accurately. Third, the type and weight of the arrow point is also a basic consideration. Archery manufacturers have designed sophisticated devices to measure spine, and there are charts with norms or standards available to assist the archer in matching arrows to the proper bow. A heavier arrow with a heavy arrow point will generally require stiffer spine. This is very common in the area of bow hunting. An archer should not be satisfied with generalities, however, when selecting arrows for the bow. Correct spine can mean the difference between a score of 9 and a complete miss in a target archery tournament or between killing a deer and a lost arrow during a bow-hunting season. The technical matching of arrow spine to the proper bow is another reason why the archer should purchase tackle from a professional archery shop.

Fletching

The feathers of an arrow are known collectively as fletching. Its fletching is as important to an arrow as the tail assembly is to an airplane. The function of the two analogous parts is essentially the same. They both serve to stabilize airborne objects. Fletching stabilizes an arrow by channeling, as much as possible, the wind currents encountered by the arrow during flight. Inflight equilibrium is maintained, in part, by a high velocity rotation of the arrow around the longitudinal axis of the shaft.

One of the most common forms of fletching is turkey feathers. Plastic and rubber are also being used more commonly. Most archers prefer three-fletch arrows. Three-vane turkey feather fletching is good for use in target archery. Feathers 3 to 3½ inches in length should be used by beginners. It is recommended that fletching be lengthened to 5 or 6 inches for use in bow-hunting situations. The added length is needed due to the difference in weight between target and broadhead points. The latter type of point is used in bow hunting. The larger fletching is needed to add flight stability for the heavier hunting arrow.

Figure 1.3 shows fletching variations on hunting, target, field, and bow-fishing arrows. The fletch on the top arrow is 5 inches in length, and this is a hunting arrow. The next arrow is a target arrow, and the fletch is 3 inches

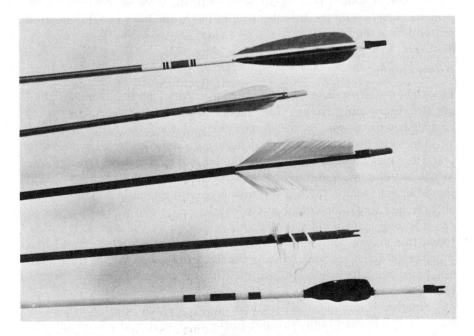

Fig. 1.3.   Fletching variations. From top to bottom: hunting, target, flu-flu, spiraled flu-flu, and rubber fishing fletching.

in length. The large fletching on the middle arrow is 5½ inches in length, and that type of fletch is designed to increase the drag resistance on a field or bow-hunting arrow. Obviously, these arrows will not fly as far if a target is missed. Therefore, they are not lost as frequently by field archers or bow hunters. The next arrow shows a spiraled flu-flu fletch, and this type of fletching is also designed to increase air resistance so arrows will not travel as far in flight. The bottom arrow is an example of rubber fletching on a bow-fishing arrow. Fletching is not very important on bow-fishing arrows, because the arrow simply does not have to fly very far to reach its intended target.

Fletching is usually colored in a distinct and traditional manner. On a three-fletched arrow, two vanes will be drab in color and one vane will usually be rather flamboyant. The bright or odd-colored feather is known as the "index feather," and is placed at a ninety-degree angle to the slit in the nock of the arrow. This can be seen in the upper two arrows in figure 1.3.

The index feather traditionally is placed so it points outward from the bow when the arrow is nocked or placed in the bowstring. It is recommended that experienced archers try shooting periodically on an experimental basis with the index feather downward or toward the bow. Flight patterns shot both ways should be evaluated. The best technique of fletching placement should be adopted permanently after a satisfactory evaluation. Most archers do prefer that the index feather be placed so it does point outward from the bow.

Arrow Length

Length of the arrow varies for each individual. Arm length and anchor point are the determining factors. *The anchor point is the placement of the archer's bowstring hand on the chin or face with the bow at full draw.*

One way to determine arrow length is to draw an over-length arrow marked in one-inch increments from the bottom of the arrow nock groove. While at full draw, note the inch mark nearest the back of the bow. That should be your arrow length if the anchor point is established. This is probably the best way to determine arrow length.

The beginner should allow an additional inch for the arrows. It will be found that anchor-point adjustments must be made as skill develops. It is much better to have arrows too long for the bow than too short. Bow hunters should also allow an additional inch for the longer and heavier broadhead point.

Another commonly used method of determining arrow length is to have the archer hold both arms out to the sides at shoulder level (abduct both shoulder joints ninety degrees). Obtain the arm spread measurement in inches from the ends of the middle fingers:

Spread Measurement	Arrow Length
57-59 inches	22-23 inches
60-62 inches	23-24 inches
63-65 inches	24-25 inches
66-68 inches	25-26 inches
69-71 inches	26-27 inches
72-74 inches	27-28 inches
75-77 inches	28-29 inches
78+ inches	30 inches

Arrow Points

Arrow points are manufactured in a wide variety of assortments and sizes. Target archery and field archery points are fairly standardized, but you will find a great variety of bow-hunting and bow-fishing points. The beginning archer should start with light points for target archery (fig. 1.4). After the fundamentals of target archery are learned new arrow points may be purchased for such things as field archery, bow hunting, or bow fishing.

Fig. 1.4. Target point.

Figure 1.5 shows a commonly used hunting arrow point or broadhead. This is a relatively heavy point when compared with the target point in figure 1.4. Blades with two or more cutting edges are increasing in popularity among bow hunters. The number of cutting surfaces is actually a matter of individual preference. The most important consideration is the sharpness of the various blades on the broadhead. *A bow-hunting arrow must be razor-sharp.* A dull hunting arrow is almost useless to the bow hunter when hunting larger game such as bear and deer.

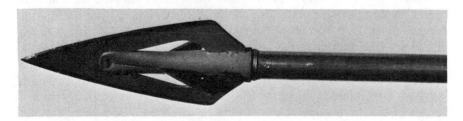

Fig. 1.5. Broadhead or hunting point.

Figure 1.6 shows a field arrow point. This style point is commonly used by field archers, and it screws into the device glued on the end of the arrow shaft. In comparison with the target point, it is relatively heavy; consequently, larger fletching is often required on field archery arrows as compared to target archery arrows.

Fig. 1.6.   Field Point.

Figure 1.7 shows a commonly used bow-fishing point. There are many different styles of fishing points on the market. Most of them are equipped with a barb type of arrangement whereby the fish is unable to pull free once the arrow has found its mark. Unlike fiberglass arrow shafts used for target archery, bow-fishing fiberglass shafts are solid. This factor, plus the weight of the fishing point, makes the arrow relatively heavy. Some bow-fishing arrows are equipped with rubber fletching, and others are not equipped with any fletching.

Fig. 1.7.   Fishing Point.

THE BOW

The bow has fascinated men throughout history. They have used it for killing animals and their enemies, making music, drilling holes in the ground, and for sport.

Bows have been built in all sizes and shapes. As examples, some archers in the Far East have used seven-foot bows with straight, uneven limbs; some African tribes use a three-foot bow with straight, even limbs; Englishmen of the eleventh century used a bow five feet long with straight limbs. Warriors at the Temple of Aigina used bows with duo-flexed limbs; the Navajo Indians of the southwestern United States used a crude, short bow for hunting purposes; modern target archery champions prefer working recurve bows and takedown bows like or similar to the bows shown in figures 1.8 and 1.9.

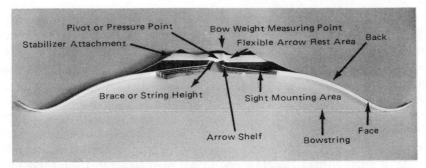

Fig. 1.8. Bow terminology (Courtesy Black Widow Bows, Springfield Missouri 65807).

Fig.1.9. A take-down recurve bow (Courtesy Black Widow Bows, Springfield, Missouri 65807).

Which type of bow is most efficient? There have been many arguments on this subject; however, current evidence leads to the conclusion that a well-constructed working recurve bow is the most efficient on the market. As one example, the Black Widow Bow manufactured by Wilson Brothers, of Springfield, Missouri, is an excellent and highly efficient multipurpose working recurve bow which now is manufactured in a takedown model as seen in figure 1.9. There are many other highly efficient working recurve bows on the market from which the archer can choose. Quality bows for top-flight competitive purposes in target archery will range from $150 to $225 each.

A working recurve bow can be identified by observing the position of the bowstring on the face of the bow. The working recurve bow will have the string lying on the face of the bow for at least two inches at each end of the limbs. This feature greatly enhances the leverage potential of the bow and the subsequent velocity of the arrow.

There has been a decided change in recent years regarding bow construction. The bow shown in figure 1.8 was constructed of laminated fiberglass and hard rock maple with the handle sections of Brazilian rosewood. This is a very efficient type of bow which will last the archer through many years of shooting if cared for properly. However, bowyers and archery manufacturers have turned to an even more efficient bow design. The most commonly constructed bow today is the takedown bow as shown in figure 1.9. Figure 1.10 shows how simple it is to assemble—to attach the handle or riser section to the limbs. This type of bow has greater stability than the older laminated type of construction. For one thing, the takedown bow as shown in figures 1.9 and 1.10 has a greater mass weight than the older laminated fiberglass and wood bows. The mass weight, for example, will exceed four pounds, especially when a stabilizer is attached. This is a positive factor for shooting purposes, benefiting the stronger archer; however, it can very well be a distinct disadvantage for the individual who does not have adequate muscular strength and muscular endurance in the shoulder joint-shoulder girdle area of the bow arm. Another advantage of the takedown bow is the fact that limb length can be changed if desired. Bow lengths usually range from sixty-five to sixty-nine inches depending upon the bow model.

A quality bow has a section cut away at the midline of its upper limb. This is called center shot design. The cutaway area is used as the sight window. This feature minimizes the components of the Archer's Paradox, because the arrow is able to move past the bow in a relatively close path to the bow string alignment with the face of the bow. Another very important feature of a bow with center shot design is the practical aspect of allowing the archer to see the intended target.

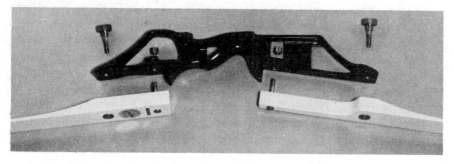

Fig. 1.10.   Assembly of the riser to the limbs on a take-down bow (Courtesy Black Widow Bows, Springfield, Missouri 65807).

Bow Weight

The weight of the bow is very important. Bow weight is defined as the bow manufacturers' determination of the number of pounds required to draw the bowstring a given distance—usually twenty-eight inches. Mass weight of the bow, as discussed above, is the literal weight of the bow in pounds and should not be confused with draw weight.

Due to the force potential of the recurve bow, a functional bow weight may be chosen within the range of thirty to forty-five pounds for men. Most experienced women archers prefer bow weights from twenty to thirty pounds. These bow weights are functional for target archery, bow hunting, and field archery.

As indicated, bow weights are determined according to the number of pounds required to pull the bowstring back to full draw for a given arrow length. Most bows are marked for bow weight at a twenty-eight-inch draw. As the draw diminishes in length, the bow weight also diminishes in pounds. Conversely, as the draw increases in length, the bow weight increases in pounds. The archer needs to know the actual draw weight for the arrow length being pulled. The recommended procedure for doing this was established by the Archery Manufacturer's Organization. This fairly simple procedure is accomplished as follows: Divide the draw weight marked on the bow by twenty, and determine how many inches, more or less, the actual draw length deviates from twenty-eight inches. Multiply these two answers, and subtract (or add) the answer from the weight marked on the bow. The result of this simple calculation gives the archer the actual draw weight. As an example, assume that an archer has a thirty-five-pound bow, and is actually drawing thirty inches. Thirty-five divided by twenty equals 1.75. In this example, 1.75 would be multiplied by two, which is the extra number of inches being drawn above the twenty-eight-inch mark. The resultant answer of 3.50 would be added to the thirty-five-pound bow weight. Therefore, an archer drawing a thirty-inch arrow on a bow marked thirty-five pounds for a twenty-eight-inch draw would actually be drawing 38.5 pounds.

A beginner should learn while using a lighter bow. It is easier to learn shooting fundamentals with the lighter weight rather than with the very heavy bow. The novice should use a bow weight somewhere between twenty and twenty-five pounds during the learning process. As skill increases, bow weight may be increased proportionately. Muscular strength and muscular endurance in the shoulder-shoulder girdle areas are also important considerations in this respect.

Many archers, particularly some uninformed bow hunters and immature boys, like to believe they need a very heavy bow weight. Let us consider what actually happens when the potential kinetic energy of a bow is doubled. What are the differences in terms of arrow velocity between forty-five- and ninety-pound bows? Will arrow velocity be doubled? Tripled? Taking variable arrow weights into consideration, it has been established that a ninety-pound bow only increases arrow velocity between nineteen and twenty-five percent over a bow weight of forty-five pounds. When an archer considers such factors as ease of handling, shooting over prolonged periods of time during tournaments, and accuracy difficulties, is a high bow weight really worth the extra effort needed to draw it? Most archers would answer this question in the negative.

Let us consider some of the basic differences between the working recurve bow and the older long bow. This discussion is presented, because, unfortunately, some long bows are still being issued for learning purposes in some university classes. First, it should be noted that all bows sold as recurve bows do not have recurve actions. In order to work efficiently, it should be remembered that the bowstring of the recurve bow must actually touch the face of the bow for two to three inches at the end of both limbs. If the bow is not designed in this manner, it will respond essentially the same as the long bow. When the bowstring touches the recurve tips as shown in the bows in figures 1.8 and 1.9, this does increase the leverage potential and adds to arrow velocity. A recurve bow of forty-five pounds will project an arrow at a rate of speed approximately twenty percent greater than a long bow of comparable weight. A working recurve bow tends to draw more smoothly than a long bow. This is particularly true of the modern takedown bow. These bows have very little increase of weight during the last few inches of draw. The phenomenon of ever-increasing weight as one draws the bowstring hand toward the face is known as "stacking." Due to the increased arrow velocity, which is derived through increased leverage, the working recurve bow tends to project the arrow on a flatter trajectory than a long bow. This aids accuracy considerably. Finally, the semicircular configuration of a long bow seen as it is being drawn tends to cause an uneven distribution of stress in the limbs. This factor also detracts from the overall efficiency and longevity of the long bow. This stress factor within the limbs does not occur within a good working recurve bow. Except for those in the hands of expert archers who have been using long bows throughout their lifetimes, the long bow should be retired to the museum! A beginning archer should definitely learn to shoot while using a good, working recurve bow.

Bow Length

Bows are manufactured in lengths ranging from fifty-two to seventy-two inches. The popularity of the shorter bows seems to be on the decline. Many bow hunters purchase shorter bows especially for hunting purposes. The fallacy of this will be discussed in chapter 4. Many archers who start out with short bows tend to trade them for bows ranging in length from sixty-four to seventy inches. Bows of these lengths can be used effectively for both hunting and target archery. There is really no need to purchase a hunting bow less than sixty inches in length.

Inaccuracies in shooting can occur because of faulty equipment as well as from human error. Are you aware of the points to check in order to obtain the best performance from your equipment?

Many target archers use bows ranging from sixty-two to seventy inches in length. If the archer uses the traditional three-finger grip, the added length minimizes the pressure exerted by the bowstring fingers on the nock of the arrow at the time of release. In addition, the longer bows actually have greater mass weight. As indicated, this factor helps the conditioned archer to have a steadier bow hand while shooting.

The length of the draw is also a basic consideration for an individual selecting a target bow:

1. 27-inch draw—62-inch bow recommended
2. 28-inch draw—64-inch bow recommended
3. 29-inch draw—66-inch bow recommended
4. 30- and 31-inch draws—68-inch bow recommended
5. Most hunting bows are designed to take draws up to 31 inches in length

Stabilizers

One or more stabilizers can be mounted on a bow. The stabilizer can contribute to more efficient arrow flight by minimizing or negating some of the archer's fundamental shooting faults involving the bow arm. A stable bow means less twist or torque of the bow at and following release. A stabilizer is shown mounted on a target bow in figure 1.11. The stabilizer is a metal rod screwed into the back of the bow on the bow handle. The stabilizer can be adjusted for length to fit the personal preference of the archer. The number, weight, and length of stabilizers is a matter of individual preference.

A word of advice is in order regarding the use of stabilizers. *The beginner should learn basic fundamentals of shooting before mounting a stabilizer on the bow.* After the fundamentals have been learned to the extent that the archer is grouping arrows consistently, a stabilizer can then be used for a portion of all future practice sessions. However, the archer should try to correct fundamental faults without using the stabilizer. If successfully done, this will mean higher scores when the stabilizer is used in competitive situations. A stabilizer should not be used as a "crutch" to compensate for fundamental faults.

Fig. 1.11. Bow equipped with one stabilizer.

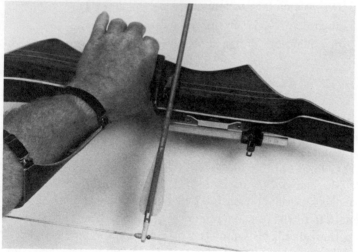

Fig. 1.12.   Bowstring, serving, and nock-locators.

Bowstrings

Like arrows, bowstrings must be matched and fitted to specific bows. The archery manufacturer will make definite recommendations regarding which bowstring to use with a designed bow. Bowstrings are made of Dacron strands. The number of strands used is dependent upon bow weight. As examples, bows ranging in weight from twenty to thirty pounds should have bowstrings of eight strands. Bows having weights from thirty-five to forty-five pounds should be equipped with twelve-strand bowstrings. Bowstrings can be adjusted or shortened by twisting. However, this technique should be limited to a maximum of twelve twists to minimize friction and strand breakage within the string.

The middle portion of the bowstring is called the serving. The arrow is placed on the string or nock at a point on the serving. As can be seen in figure 1.12, two nock-locaters have been mounted on the serving. The nock-locaters tend to serve as the stop on the serving of the bowstring which marks the exact nocking point for the arrow. These locaters insure that the exact nocking angle will be consistent from shot to shot. The added thread wrapping around the portion of the bowstring known as the serving is needed to protect the string from breakage, because this area of the bow-string receives considerable wear and tear.

Bowsights

Figures 1.13 and 1.14 show two types of commonly-used bowsights.

Fig. 1.13. Accra bowsight mounted on the bow face.

Fig. 1.14. Level bowsight mounted on the bow face.

Sights are usually mounted on the face of the bow immediately above the arrow rest. Some archers, however, prefer to mount sights on the back of the bow. The mounting sight preference relates mainly to the individual's visual acuity. There are numerous commercial bowsights on the market, and these range from inexpensive models such as those shown in figures 1.13 and 1.14 to very expensive prism sights manufactured by optical companies. The type of sight used depends upon the objectives of the archer and specific rules in various types of competition related to bowsights.

The beginner is encouraged to use a bowsight for aiming purposes. Bowsights are being used extensively in target archery tournaments and free-style shooting in field archery. Furthermore, bowsights are being used considerably by bow hunters.

ACCESSORIES

The archer must have protection for the bow arm and bowstring fingers. The bow arm must be protected from possible contusions due to being slapped by the bowstring in the general region of the radioulnar and wrist joints. Without protection, the bowstring fingers become severely irritated due to the constant pressure and friction exerted by the bowstring. Two common leather accessories, the finger tab and arm guard, are shown in figures 1.15 and 1.16. Both come in several sizes, shapes, and styles. These accessories are relatively inexpensive.

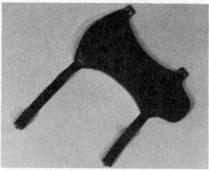

Fig. 1.15. Finger tab (Courtesy Wilson Brothers).

Fig. 1.16. Arm guard.

The finger tab is rather awkward to use at first, but it is absolutely essential for prolonged shooting during class or tournaments while using the conventional three-finger release technique. Tender skin may become blistered by the friction created when the bowstring rolls over the fingertips if a finger tab is not used. This, of course, would have an adverse effect on accuracy.

Many archers prefer shooting gloves instead of finger tabs. A shooting glove is shown in figure 2.15.

The arm guard is placed on the bow arm between the elbow and wrist. The arm guard is shown in figures 1.16 and 1.18. The lower arm in the vicinity of the wrist is an area which is "slapped" periodically by the bowstring when it is released. Shooting without an arm guard can result in serious contusions. Furthermore, following one severe blow by the bowstring on an unprotected arm, an archer has a tendency to flinch—flexion occurs in the elbow and/or wrist—when the arrow is released. These movements at the elbow and wrist are bad habits which the protection afforded by the arm guard tends to eliminate.

A finger sling is an accessory that can also help eliminate some problems during release and follow-through. The finger sling is shown in figures 1.17 and 1.18. The finger sling attaches to the index or middle finger and

Fig. 1.17.   Finger sling.

Fig. 1.18.   Arm guard and finger sling in use.

the thumb of the bow hand. It then extends across the back of the bow as shown in figure 1.18. It serves the purpose of keeping the bow from falling to the ground during release of the arrow and the subsequent follow-through. Therefore, the archer can concentrate more on the release and less on losing control of the bow.

An arrow quiver is another accessory which the archer must obtain. This is a device designed to carry arrows. There are shoulder, hip, ground, pocket, and bow quivers available. These come in all sizes, shapes, prices, and materials. Most beginners rely upon inexpensive, ground quivers. The most commonly-used quiver, however, is the hip quiver as shown in figures 1.11 and 1.19. The bow quiver seems to be gaining in popularity among bow hunters, because it does attach to the bow and eliminates carrying an extra object. Furthermore, the bow quiver makes the arrows more accessible to

Fig. 1.19. Hip quiver.

the bow hunter for that possible second shot at the game animal. A bow quiver is shown in figure 1.18.

Another important accessory is the arrow rest. This is a small device mounted just above the arrow shelf on the bow to maintain arrow position from nocking to release. Figures 1.20 and 1.21 show the arrow rest with and without the arrow in position. Contrary to a belief popularly held by beginning archers, the arrow shelf of the bow should not be used to hold arrows

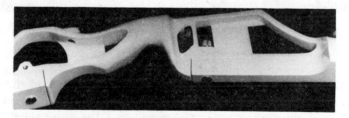

Fig. 1.20.   Arrow rest without an arrow.

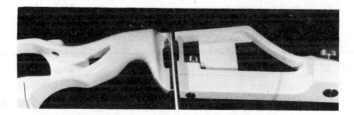

Fig. 1.21.   Arrow rest with the arrow at full draw.

What criterion must be met for a recurve bow to be judged more efficient than a long bow?

---

during the nocking, drawing, and release procedures. Placing the arrow on the arrow shelf of the bow would lead to many inconsistencies in accuracy.

CARE OF ARCHERY TACKLE

The Bow

The following care and treatment of a bow will add to its longevity and effectiveness.

1. Always unstring the bow after use with a bowstringer.
2. Place the bow in a bow case for storage purposes. In the case of a take-down bow, remove the bow limbs prior to inserting it in the bow case.
3. Lay the bow in a flat place or hang it vertically if a bow case is not available.
4. To protect the outer surface of the bow, wax it periodically.
5. Use beeswax on the bowstring occasionally to minimize fraying.
6. Do not leave the bow lying on the ground when retrieving arrows from the target.
7. Do not drop the bow.
8. Draw the bow several times to your draw length prior to actually shooting an arrow, but do not release the string at full draw without an arrow in the bow.
9. Always use a bowstringer to brace the bow.

Arrows

The following care and treatment of arrows will add to their longevity and effectiveness:

1. Store arrows in an arrow case.
2. Wipe arrows clean after shooting.
3. Check fletching periodically and replace as needed. Fletching can be replaced at a very low cost.
4. Check fletching periodically and replace damaged fletching. placed.
5. Do not carry arrows in a tightly clenched fist. This tends to damage fletching. Place the arrows between the fingers when carrying them back from the target to the shooting line.

Fundamentals
of target archery

2

Practicing archery fundamentals in front of a target is absolutely essential for achieving future success in target archery tournaments, bow hunting, field archery, and other archery events. As in any other sport, basic techniques of archery have been modified by individuals and champions. Archers have many theories, preferences, and styles of shooting. These have been developed through years of competition and practice. However, the basic fundamentals of archery, which are accepted as the stereotype of perfect form for beginners, are discussed in this chapter. Variations or modifications of basic form and style are mentioned on occasions. The beginner may want to try these variations, but this should be done only *after* becoming familiar with tackle and basic shooting techniques.

NOTE: All discussions and illustrations in this textbook pertain to the right-handed archer.

ARCHERY AND SAFETY

The archer should keep the following concept in mind when archery tackle is in hand: *Archery is not a dangerous sport, but the bow and arrow does have lethal potential.* As a consequence, respect should be shown for one's tackle and other human beings while on an archery range of any kind.

Safety rules vary from range to range. All rules, however, incorporate good common sense with the concept of always being aware of the whereabouts of your fellow archers. When an arrow is placed in a bow it should be pointed *only* in the direction of the intended target. The archer must know beyond all doubt that no other human being is within arrow distance of the intended target. This is easier to ascertain on target archery ranges than on field archery ranges or in bow-hunting situations. Each archery instructor will post and announce range safety rules. When these safety rules are followed in detail, archery is one of the safest of all sports.

The archer should go to the range in comfortable clothing. Loose fitting golf sweaters, long-sleeved shirts, and blouses are not recommended clothing to be worn on the archery range. That type of clothing can become entangled with the bowstring after it has been released. Also, watches should not be worn on the bow arm while shooting.

BRACING

Bracing the bow simply means attaching the bowstring to the bow in preparation for shooting. Bracing the bow can create problems for some archers, and it must be remembered that bows can also be damaged due to improper bracing techniques. Working recurve bows should always be braced with a bowstringer. If a bow is broken while using the older push-pull and step-through methods of bracing, some bow manufacturers will not replace the broken bows under their guarantees.

A bowstringer is shown in figure 2.1. Figures 2.2 and 2.3 show how to use the bowstringer. The bowstringer shown in figure 2.1 is equipped with two leather pockets, one longer than the other. Place the longer leather pocket on the lower tip of the bow, and place the shorter pocket on the upper tip of the bow. Turn the bow face downward, and place the left foot on the center of the bowstringer (fig. 2.2). Grip the bow firmly, and pull it straight upward. At the same time, slide the loose loop of the bowstring

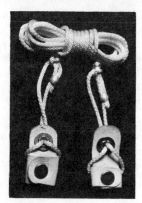

Fig. 2.1.   Bowstringer
(Courtesy of Bow-Pal).

Fig. 2.2. Bracing with a bow-stringer—Step one.

Fig. 2.3. Bracing with a bow-stringer—Step two.

into its notch (fig. 2.3). Check both bow notches to see that the bowstring is properly inserted prior to shooting. To unstring the bow, the above procedure is reversed. The use of a bowstringer is simple, safe, and recommended at all times.

If, however, a bowstringer is not available, there are two methods for bracing a bow manually: (1) the push-pull method and (2) the step-through method. The method used by the archer depends upon the weight of the bow, design of the bow, and strength of the individual.

For most lightweight bows and archers with average strength, the push-pull method of bracing is adequate. The following is the procedure for using the push-pull method of bracing:

1. Place the lower limb of the bow against the instep of the right foot; be certain that the bowstring is placed in the notch on the lower limb of the bow.

2. Grasp the handle with the right hand.

3. Grasp the loop of the bowstring with the thumb and index finger of the left hand and slide it up the lower limb toward the notch of the bow.

4. PULL with the right hand and PUSH down on the upper limb with the left hand while sliding the bowstring upward and into the bow

notch. *For safety purposes, keep your face out of alignment with the upper limb.*

5. Check to see that both bowstring loops are properly inserted (fully) into each bow nocks. This is a final safety precaution.

The step-through method of bracing is used more frequently than the push-pull method, especially with working recurve bows. However, this bracing technique is only recommended when a bowstringer is not available for the archer:

1. Assume an upright stance with the feet apart at shoulder width.
2. Step through or between the bowstring and face of the bow with the right leg.
3. See that the recurve of the lower bow limb encircles your left ankle.
4. Taking advantage of the leverage which this bow position allows, grasp the upper bow limb and bend it forward and downward with the right hand.
5. Move the bowstring upward, placing it in the bow notch with the left hand as the upper limb is being bent downward.
6. Check both bow notches to see that bowstring loops are properly inserted into each. Failure to insert them properly exposes the archer to danger during the shooting process.

If the bow should slip during this step-through procedure for bracing, cuffs of slacks, pantyhose, and trousers can be ripped. Steady pressure should be exerted and proper placement of the recurve around the left ankle must be checked to prevent the occurrence of that type of problem. Also, if the bow is twisted during this bracing method, it is possible to crack the bow. As can be seen in figure 2.4, variations of this bracing method have been around for a considerable period of time! If you have ever tried this bracing method while fully clothed, you might readily understand why the archer in figure 2.4 is bracing in the nude.

The actual distance from the bowstring to the handle of the bow is very important. This is known as the brace or string height. Bowyers, individuals who make bows, indicate exactly what the brace height should be for each bow. This will depend upon the length of the bow. As one example, the manufacturer's recommended string height for the bow in figure 2.2 is 9¾ to 10¾ inches for a 69-inch bow and 9½ to 10½ inches for a 67-inch bow. The archer should measure the string height accurately after the bow has been braced. A bowstring too close or too far from the face of the bow will adversely affect arrow velocity and flight. The bowstring can be turned or twisted in order to make adjustments for proper string heights, but the

Fig. 2.4. A Scythian archer in the act of bracing his bow. Since early times this method has proved satisfactory for stringing short and powerful composite bows. From a kylix by the Paraitois painter, after c. 490 B.C. (From E. G. Heath, **The Grey Goose Wing).**

twists of the string should be limited to a range of three to ten twists for any single adjustment. If more are required, a properly fitting bowstring should be acquired.

STANCE

The right-handed archer stands with the left side of the body toward the intended target. The archer's stance must be consistent from shot to shot. The exact placement of the feet on the shooting line should be marked. Golf tees provide good markers for this purpose. They can be driven into the ground to indicate heel and toe placement for both feet. This type of procedure enables the archer to return to the exact stance on the shooting line after retrieving arrows. Stance deviations of even a few inches can cause sighting and aiming problems which in turn lead to accuracy problems. Consistency is a key word in the sport of target archery.

Figures 2.5, 2.6, 2.7, and 2.8 show four different types of foot placement which can be used by archers.

Many archers prefer the even stance shown in figure 2.5. In this stance, the shooting line is straddled and weight is evenly distributed over both feet. As can be seen, the heels and toes of the feet are aligned, and the middle of the instep of the foot should be aligned with the center of the intended target. The archer in figure 2.9 is addressing the target while using an even stance.

The open stance is shown in figure 2.6 and is recommended for the beginning archer during the initial learning period. The feet should be shoulder-width apart in the open stance. It is recommended that the body weight be distributed evenly on both feet. The archer should stand with both feet in such a position that an imaginary line can be drawn through the

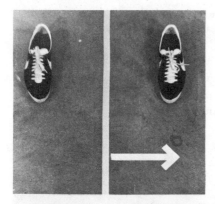

Fig. 2.5.   Even Stance.

Fig. 2.6.   Open Stance.

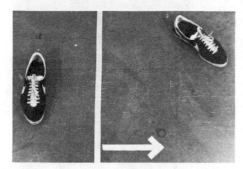

Fig. 2.7.   Oblique Stance.

Fig. 2.8.   Closed Stance.

insteps to the center of the gold on the target face, as is the case in the even stance. To "open the stance," the left foot should be moved backwards approximately six inches as shown. This stance is preferred by many archers over the even or closed stances.

Some expert archers use what is called the oblique stance as shown in figure 2.7. This stance is attained by placing the toe of the left foot nearest the target on a line with the target and pivoting the left foot so it is at a forty-five-degree angle to the target. The heel of the right foot is then placed in line with the toe of the left foot. The oblique stance allows the bow arm to remain in such a position that there will be optimum clearance of the bowstring when the arrow is released. Furthermore, with the weight distributed over the balls of the feet, total body equilibrium is enhanced. The archer in figure 2.10 is using a modified form of the oblique stance.

A closed stance is shown in figure 2.8. The shooting line is straddled and the weight is evenly distributed over both feet. The left foot is simply moved forward a few inches so that a heel-toe relationship exists between the left and right feet respectively. This type of stance is not very popular among archers.

It is recommended that the beginning archer learn while using the open stance. After you have become cognizant of all of the archery fundamentals and have had opportunities to practice, various stances should be tried during the shooting process. The final stance chosen should be the one allowing the greatest degree of comfort, stability, and accuracy for the individual.

Fig. 2.9. Addressing the target—even stance straddling the shooting line.

Fig. 2.10. Nocking the arrow—oblique stance.

NOCKING

Nocking the arrow is placement of the arrow in shooting position on the bowstring. This is an important step in preparation for shooting. In target archery, this is accomplished when all archers have assumed their stances on the shooting line. The archer holds the bow horizontal to the ground next to the hip nearest the target, as shown in figure 2.10. The arrow shaft is laid on the arrow rest. The arrow nock is placed on the bowstring with the index feather upward at the serving. Bowstrings should be equipped with rubber, metal, or plastic nocking points to insure consistency of arrow placement on the string during nocking.

How could this even stance be changed to an open stance? Why do you suppose the open stance is recommended for beginners?

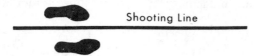

Shooting Line

The archer should start by nocking the arrow so a ninety-degree angle is formed between the arrow and bowstring. This is the traditional nocking angle (fig. 2.11). If consistent vertical fluctuations are noted in the flight pattern of arrows after several weeks of practice, the archer might try moving the nocking point upward or downward one-eighth to one-quarter of an inch. This adjustment may help correct the arrow flight problems IF release techniques are perfect.

Fig. 2.11. Traditional ninety degree nocking angle.

BOW HOLD

When used in conjunction with the bow hand, terms such as "holding" and "gripping" are misnomers. They tend to be misleading as far as archery skill is concerned. The archer does not hold or grip the bow as the draw is made. The bow is held while nocking and after the arrow reaches the target. During the process of shooting, the bow is actually pushed by the bow hand at the pivot point of the bow. Consequently, the following principle should be observed: *The bow should never be gripped or held tightly during the drawing and aiming phases of shooting.* The lack of a firmly held grip on the bow during drawing and aiming tends to minimize torque when the arrow is released.

As can be seen in figures 2.12 and 2.13, the bow is placed between the thumb and index finger. The palm of the hand should not apply pressure to the bow. The index finger wraps around the bow. Some archers like to have the thumb and index fingers actually touch each other, but this is not absolutely necessary. The three remaining fingers on the bow hand should remain relaxed in a semi-extended position. Why? This tends to lessen fatigue in several muscles within the hand and forearm. Muscle tremor is reduced and this enhances accuracy. Hand placement on the bow must also be consistent. Figures 2.12 and 2.13 also show a finger sling in use. The finger sling is a very valuable asset in shooting. The finger sling is placed on the thumb and index or middle finger and wraps around the back of the bow. The sling enables the archer to release the arrow without worrying about the bow falling to the ground. Extraneous actions of the wrist joint are thereby minimized. The bow can be held literally after the archer sees the arrow embedded in the target.

Fig. 2.12.   Bow hold.

Fig. 2.13.   Bow hold—hand pressure is exerted at the pivot point.

DRAWING

Drawing is the act of pulling the bowstring to the anchor point on the archer's face. This is analogous to cocking a pistol prior to firing a bullet. One major difference is that there are many more opportunities for human error while drawing a bowstring than while cocking a pistol. Drawing may start as soon as the arrow is nocked properly. A deep breath should be taken and exhaled just before the draw is started. The breath is then held from the time the draw is started until the arrow reaches the target. The total elapsed time for breath-holding should be no more than ten seconds for most archers.

Figure 2.14 shows the very simple one-quarter turn of the archer's head toward the intended target. This seemingly simple aspect of left cervical spine rotation tends to be a definite problem for some beginning archers. It shouldn't be if the following principle is observed: *The bowstring must be drawn to the head instead of moving the head to the bowstring.* Some beginners do move the head forward or flex the neck to meet the bowstring as it is being drawn. Such practices only complicate matters. The head must remain in the position shown in figure 2.14 at all times during the process of drawing, release, and follow-through.

One excellent way to maintain head position is to mount a level on the bow. Some bowsights come equipped with level bubbles mounted on them. Such a sight is shown in figure 1.14. If the bubble is off center, the archer should maintain the bow in a vertical position and adjust the head angle to fit the bow and string.

Figure 2.15 shows the commonly used three-finger bowstring grip. A shooting glove is being used to protect the bow fingers. The little finger and

Fig. 2.14. Head rotation while addressing the target.

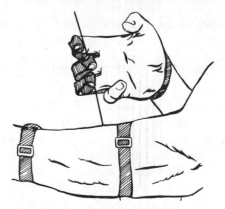

Fig. 2.15. Traditional three finger grip with shooting glove.

thumb do not touch the bowstring. The remaining three fingers are placed on the bowstring at the level of the distal finger joints, i.e., the bowstring is placed in the crease formed by the first finger joints. The distal and middle joints of the three fingers are flexed as the draw is made. *It must be noted that the large knuckle joints of the hand are not flexed at any time during the draw. These joints remain extended at all times.* In addition, the wrist is maintained in a straight or extended position throughout the draw and release phases. The wrist never flexes or hyperextends during the draw and release.

Figure 2.16 shows the relationship between the index and middle fingers and the nock of the arrow while using a finger tab. Although this appears to be simple, position of the fingers on the bowstring next to the arrow nock is difficult to maintain as the pressure increases during the draw. The essence of the problem lies in the nature of the musculature within the hand. As fingers are flexed, it is natural for them to be drawn tightly together into a fist. This is fine for the boxer, but it creates arrow flight

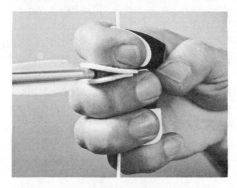

Fig. 2.16. Arrow-finger tab relationship (Courtesy Wilson Brothers).

problems for the archer! Because the index and middle fingers are flexed and the pressure increases during the draw, the two fingers have a tendency to apply pressure on the arrow nock. Beginning archers find that the point of their arrows will wave around and fall completely off the arrow rest as the draw is made. This common problem is caused by finger pressure on the arrow nock. The archer must compensate for the gripping effect of the hand musculature prior to the draw by placing the index finger one-eighth of an inch above the arrow nock. The middle finger is placed the same distance below the arrow nock. It may seem that the arrow will become disengaged from the bowstring before the draw can be made, but this feeling will be eliminated by the use of nocking points and practice. The principle to bear in mind is: *Pressure exerted by fingers on the arrow nock should be kept at an absolute minimum prior to the draw.*

The problem of pressure against the arrow nock exerted by fingers during the draw process is completely eliminated when using a release aid. This is one reason release aids have been banned in target archery. A great portion of the sport of target archery is the ability of the archer to control this type of pressure from draw to release. Release aids eliminate a tremendous amount of human error but, in the process, they also negate many of the aspects of target archery as a complex sport. Release aids can be used in the sport of bow hunting and will be discussed in chapter 4.

As the draw is made, the bow is moved from a horizontal to a vertical position. The archer in figure 2.17 is starting the draw. The bowstring hand is being pulled toward the face. As this is being accomplished, the bow hand is relatively relaxed on the bow. It is being held in position by the force being exerted backwards by the right arm. The act of drawing a bow is actually a force-counterforce situation. The completed draw is shown in figure 2.18.

The position of the bow arm is very important. During the draw the bow arm is raised to shoulder height. The wrist and elbow should be extended and stabilized when the archer has drawn the arrow to the anchor point. The shoulder should remain stable or unmoving during the aiming and release phases. When the arrow is released, the bow arm will react by moving downward.

Fig. 2.17. Start of the draw. To clearly illustrate finger position, a finger tab was not used.

Fig. 2.18. Completed draw. To clearly illustrate finger position, a finger tab was not used.

The bowstring should not slap the bow arm after it has been released if the bow arm position is correct. The arm guard may be hit periodically. This can be caused by any extra shoulder, elbow, or wrist movements. "String slaps" will diminish in frequency as the archer increases in skill. Some archers, however, do require adjustments of their body positions to eliminate painful contusions caused by continued "string slaps" on the bow arm. If the bowstring hits the bow arm above the arm guard, the archer's stance probably should be changed to the oblique stance described previously. For most individuals this should eliminate the problem. If such a stance adjustment does not work, a bow arm adjustment should be made. The arm should always remain abducted at the shoulder joint and extended at the elbow joint as shown in figure 2.18. To make the bow arm adjustment the bow should be held in a position horizontal to the ground initially. Slowly rotate the bow to the vertical position by laterally rotating the bow shoulder —move the bow counterclockwise—with the elbow extended. This should pull the arm out of the path of the bowstring. If this does not work, medially rotate the shoulder of the bow arm—clockwise rotation of the bow—at the shoulder. *One should never flex the elbow to allow the string to clear the arm.*

ANCHOR POINT

The term "anchor point" means the place on an archer's face where the hand is placed with the bowstring at full draw. Anchor points are usually described as being high or low on the face (figs. 2.19 and 2.20). An anchor point on or under the mandible or jaw bone is termed low. An anchor point on or underneath the bone beneath the eye is high. Preference for a particular anchor point usually involves such factors as facial contour and type of shooting. Many field archers, bow hunters, and instinctive shooters use the high anchor point. These archers like to think they sight down the shaft of the arrow, but actually they tend to look over the arrow point. The low anchor point is used very often by target archers who rely on bowsights for aiming. Both types of anchor points can be used effectively for any kind of shooting. The archer ultimately should use the anchor point which feels most comfortable and is most consistent with good aiming.

It is recommended that the beginner utilize a low anchor point in target archery. Figure 2.20 shows a low anchor point. To learn any athletic activity, one must utilize as many senses as possible. The low anchor point involves the touch, pressure, sight, and kinesthetic (feeling) senses. The index finger is placed under the chin, and slight pressure is exerted on the man-

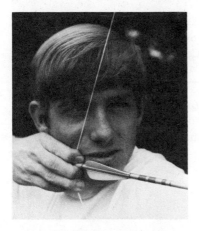

Fig. 2.19. A high anchor point
(To clearly illustrate finger position, a finger tab was not used.)

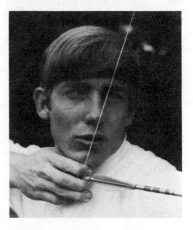

Fig. 2.20. A low anchor point
(To clearly illustrate finger position, a finger tab was not used.)

dible. The position allows the bowstring to bisect and actually touch the
chin, lips, and nose. The upper and lower teeth must touch, but they should
never be clenched. That type of tension is absolutely contraindicated in
archery. Some archers place rubber kissing buds on their bowstrings. These
are kissed each time the low anchor is set. This practice insures maximum
consistency in regard to accurate placement of the archer's low anchor
point.

Some beginning archers believe that they must change the anchor
point and length of draw when shooting from varying distances. This is a
disastrous mistake. The anchor point and draw remain constant for all distances. Adjustments for shooting varying distances is accomplished by
changing the angle of the bow arm at the shoulder joint.

AIMING

Three aiming techniques are referred to in archery literature: (1) bowsights, (2) instinctive, and (3) point-of-aim. The bowsight technique
should be mastered and used by the archer in any archery situation where
bowsights are considered legal. The instinctive technique has many limita-
tions, especially in target archery tournaments and bow-hunting situations.
The point-of-aim technique is antiquated and not recommended for use.

The beginner should not worry too much about any aiming procedure
or techniques until he or she feels comfortable while using archery tackle.

Can you nock and draw without the arrow wobbling or falling off? 3 times in succession? 5 times? consistently? Can you hold a full draw steady for 3 seconds? 5 seconds? 10 seconds?

Once this feeling is acquired, the archer should turn attention toward aiming and the grouping of arrows in smaller and smaller patterns on the target. The determination of a good anchor point and release are basic to accuracy, and both should be well established prior to an overconcern for learning an aiming technique.

Bowsight Aiming

The use of the bowsight will greatly enhance one's ability to hit the intended target; consequently, the use of a bowsight is recommended over any other aiming technique. The archer must establish a bowsight setting on the bow for each shooting distance. This requires the archer to shoot a number of ends at each distance to experiment with bowsight settings. To use a bowsight, the archer places the sighting device in the middle of the intended target—gold on a regulation target archery face—and releases the arrow properly. This procedure is repeated until several ends have been shot. The archer must continually check the grouping patterns on the target face. For example, if an archer shoots six ends of arrows at a target without changing the bowsight setting and all arrows consistently group low and left on a regulation target face, the archer must move his bowsight setting device down and left for the next series of shots in order to move the grouping into the center of the target. The principle to keep in mind for bowsight adjustments is as follows: *The bowsight is always moved in the direction of the arrow grouping error.* In the example, if the adjustment is correct and fundamentals of release are good, the next end of arrows should be grouped in or near the gold on the target face. Establishing bowsight setting requires considerable shooting and experimentation. To expect good results from bowsight setting, the archer must be fundamentally sound.

Sighting and aiming with the bow and arrow differs considerably from aiming a rifle. The rifleman tends to look down the top of the rifle barrel through a series of sights mounted on the barrel. While using the low anchor point in particular, the archer does not and should not look down the shaft of the arrow. The line of sight should be through the aiming device on the bowsight toward the intended target. The bowsight is mounted above the arrow shaft. Moreover, the bow, like the rifle, does have a rear sighting device, which goes along with a mounted bowsight. This rear sighting de-

How should the bowsight be adjusted if arrow grouping is consistent in this area? if it is down and to the right?

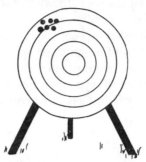

vice is the bowstring. When the archer's head is in the correct position, the archer "looks through" the string aligned down the center of the face, the bow face, and bowsight. This can be seen in figure 2.21. The bowsight is aligned with the center of the target. This procedure places the arrow in a definite direction relative to the target. The archer must be able to maintain control of the alignment between the rear sight and centered front sight if accurate aiming is to remain consistent.

There are archery authorities who contend that the eye nearest the target should always be closed during the act of shooting. This is a fallacy!

Fig. 2.21.   Bowstring pattern while aiming.

What if the eye away from the target—the right eye for a right-handed archer—is the weak eye? Should the good eye be closed and the weak eye remain open? One would logically assume that this could have a detrimental bearing upon accuracy, and accuracy is the essence of the sport of target archery. Many fine right-handed archers shoot with both eyes open or with the left eye partially closed and the right eye open. Eye preference is a highly individualized matter. It is recommended that the beginner try shooting while using all combinations of eye openings and closures. Each archer should use the eye position which feels most comfortable and produces the best results.

Instinctive Aiming

Many people who hunt with rifles and bows interchangeably use high anchor points. This allows them to partially sight down the arrow shaft and over the point if a bowsight is not used. Many bow hunters do not use a bowsight, but rely upon instinctive aiming techniques. Instinctive aiming is utilized by many field archers also. There are tournaments held in field archery for bare bow or instinctive shooters exclusively. Many excellent scores are recorded in these tournaments, and the lack of mechanical aiming devices adds to the spirit of true sport.

Each archer who uses instinctive aiming usually provides a slightly different version of how this task is accomplished. Basically, the instinctive archer must have excellent eyesight and depth perception. The term "instinct" as it is used in conjunction with this style of shooting is grossly incorrect from a scientific standpoint. Through extensive practice over a long period of time, the archer increases kinesthetic awareness, visual awareness, and archery fundamentals. (Instinct, as it is scientifically defined, has little, if anything, to do with it.) This set of factors enables the archer to adjust rapidly as he peers over the arrow point toward the target. The archer will see a gap or space between the arrow point and intended target. The release of the arrow is calculated to coincide with the arrow point's bissection of the aiming area and line of sight. The archer holds the bow arm motionless for a second at the time of release. The beginner should practice with the bowsight technique extensively prior to trying instinctive shooting.

RELEASE AND FOLLOW-THROUGH

Releasing an arrow is the most important fundamental of shooting. The key elements are: (1) relaxation and (2) concentration. The paradoxical nature of these two factors at this critical stage of shooting adds another dimension to the challenge of archery as a sport. As the reader realizes, it is extremely difficult to relax during a time of intense concentration. Both of these elements must be under complete control, however, for any degree of success in archery to be achieved.

When the traditional three-finger grip is used, releasing an arrow *is not* a result of forceful finger extension. It *is* a matter of relaxing the musculature to some extent within the bow hand and forearm. When the muscles controlling flexion within the three drawing fingers release some of their tension during contraction, the bowstring will move forward as a result of the pressure brought about by the bow weight at complete draw. The bowstring will literally brush the fingers away from its path if the fingers have been relaxed sufficiently. However, the finger extension usually will clear the string as it moves forward. The archer does very little muscular work at the time of release in terms of extending the finger joints. As stated previously, the main problems are *relaxation* of hand and forearm muscles in conjunction with maximum *concentration* on aiming prior to and at the time of release. Extreme concentration regarding the task at hand must be accomplished by the archer from the time of nocking until the arrow is released. It is too late to concentrate when the arrow is in flight!

Figure 2.22 shows proper release form without the use of a release aid. The elbow of the bowstring arm should not extend appreciably after or during the release. The bowstring hand will usually move backward in a position relatively close to the chin or neck after release. This is a natural recoil action following release. The beginner must avoid the habit of trying to release the arrow by hyperextending the wrist—moving the back of the hand toward the forearm—and allowing the bowstring to roll off the fingertips.

Fig. 2.22.   Release and follow-through positions.

This "plucking" of the string causes very erratic arrow grouping. Also, the elbow of the bowstring arm should never be extended during the release. The elbow should remain in the flexed position as shown in figure 2.22.

To follow through in archery means to hold the release position until the arrow is safely embedded in the target.

The following are features of a good follow-through: (1) the fingers on the bowstring hand are relaxed, (2) head and eyes are turned toward the target, (3) the bow arm is extended toward the target, and (4) the bow hand is gripping the bow with the help of the finger sling. Why is follow-through important? It is absolutely essential for consistent performance and minute accuracy. If there are any movements observed in the follow-through phase of shooting, those movements were probably initiated prior to and continued through the release phase. Obviously, this is contraindicated as far as archery accuracy is concerned.

Figure 2.23 shows the important phases of archery fundamentals from nocking to follow-through.

SCORING

Figure 2.24 shows two archers retrieving and scoring arrows. The regulation target archery face is forty-eight inches in diameter. It has five concentric

Fig. 2.23. Nocking through release.

rings from inside to outside colored gold (center or bull's eye), red, blue, black, and white. The respective point values for these concentric rings are nine, seven, five, three, and one. A perfect end, therefore, is worth fifty-four points. A *round* consists of a designated number of ends shot at varying distances. Using the game of baseball as an analogous example, an end would equal one inning, and nine innings or a completed game would equal a round. There are numerous standard rounds for all ages and both sexes. Some of these rounds are described in chapter 3.

In international target archery competition, a ten-ring scoring target face is utilized. The scoring values of the ten concentric circles from inside out are as follows: inner gold, ten points; outer gold, nine points; inner red, eight points; outer red, seven points; inner blue, six points; outer blue, five points; inner black, four points; outer black, three points; inner white, two points; outer white, one point.

Scoring in target archery should be done by the target captain. This individual pulls the arrows from the target. The high value arrows are always pulled first. The target captain gives the score of the arrow to the recorder who marks the score on an official score card. The recorder also indicates the number of hits on the score card for each archer.

Some scoring variations for target archery are as follows: (1) An arrow bisecting a line between colors is given the higher value of the two colors.

Fig. 2.23. (Cont'd)

(2) An arrow rebounding from the target is scored seven points, if witnessed. (3) An arrow that passes completely through the scoring face, if witnessed, is also recorded as seven points.

Pulling arrows from a target mat mounted on a tripod stand should be done with caution. The arrow should be grasped by the shaft near the target face with one hand. The other hand should be used to push against the target mat while the arrow is pulled from the target. This simple procedure eliminates the embarrassing and sometimes costly experience of pulling a target full of arrows over onto the ground.

Fig. 2.24.   Scoring. The target captain pulls the arrows and gives their values to the scorer.

As a safety precaution, the person pulling arrows from the target should check to see that no one is standing behind as the arrows are being pulled. An arrow nock in the eye can be very traumatic.

During university archery classes, easels are used in many situations to wheel target mats onto the fields. In this instance, the center of the gold is only twenty-four inches above the ground. For sanctioned archery tournaments, the center of the gold must be fifty-one inches above the ground. The target face must also be inclined away from the shooting line at an angle ranging from twelve to eighteen degrees from the vertical.

COMMON GROUPING PROBLEMS

To consistently group one's arrows in the gold of the target regardless of the distance being shot represents the ultimate in target archery. The frustration of the sport is the fact that arrows do not always group according to the desires of the archer. The main source of help in regard to consistent grouping and fundamental adjustments must come from the individual's archery instructor or coach. However, when such help is not available, the following

---

Have you mastered the scoring system using a regulation target face? What is the total score for an end in which two arrows strike the red, one the blue, two the white, and one is seen to rebound from the target? What is the score if one arrow strikes the gold, three arrows the black, one bisects the red and blue, and one is seen to pass entirely through the target?

---

teaching or *coaching suggestions* for self-help can be quite valuable. Pragmatically, the archer who does not have a teacher or coach should try the suggestions and utilize the one(s) which correct the problem. In regard to the suggestions listed below, the assumption is made that the archer is using matched tackle.

Arrows Grouping Left

1. Check your stance. You may have inadvertently rotated your body slightly to the left. Place your entire body in line with the target with good weight distribution over your stance.
2. Adjust your bowsight to the left.
3. Check your bow grip. Do not involve the fingers in the gripping process; push with the bow hand; use a finger or bow sling.
4. The anchor point may have been moved to the right. Make certain the string placement is consistently touching the same facial areas and is aligned with the center of the bow; use a kissing button on the bowstring.
5. Nock with the index feather skyward in the nocking position.
6. The bow may cant to the left during aiming and release; consequently, check to see that the bow is held perpendicular to the ground instead of being rotated counterclockwise during the shooting phases.
7. Check the position of the elbow on the bow arm; this elbow should be fully extended at all times from nocking through follow-through. You may be flinching or flexing the elbow at release.
8. Check to see that you are not applying too much pressure on the nock of the arrow during the draw and release with the index and middle fingers; allow an extra space between the gripping fingers and arrow nock.

Arrows Grouping Right

1. Check your stance; align your body with the target instead of rotating it to the right.

2. Adjust the bowsight to the right.
3. Adjust your grip to eliminate any possibility of a clockwise torque of the bow during release.
4. Check to see that your string alignment has not moved to the left; align the string to touch the middle of the nose and lips.
5. Concentrate on extension only of the finger (interphalangeal) joints during release. Any extraneous action such as plucking the string or pushing the string inward will cause a grouping error to the right.
6. Make certain that the bow is held perpendicular to the ground and not canted counterclockwise.

Arrows Grouping High

1. Check your stance for an even weight distribution as opposed to placing too much weight on the leg away from the target.
2. Adjust your bowsight upward.
3. Make certain you are not pushing against the bow grip with the entire palm or heel of the hand.
4. Keep your mouth closed; upper and lower teeth should be touching—not clenched—from the time you reach your anchor point through release; check the anchor point to see that it has not moved to a lower position on your face. The hand must maintain contact with the jaw.
5. Make certain that a ninety-degree string-arrow nock position is attained during nocking. A low nocking causes the arrow to go high. Place nocking points on your serving if they are not being used at the present time.
6. Do not inhale during the drawing, aiming, or release phases; breathing should be done before nocking, and you should exhale after the arrow is in the target.
7. Push through the bow at all times from drawing to follow-through; do not raise (abduct) the bow arm at release.
8. Take time to aim so your release will coincide with the bowsight intersecting the desired target spot instead of releasing above the target.
9. Check the bowstring fingers to make certain that the pressure is equally distributed over all three fingers.
10. Keep the wrist stabilized and extended at release so that no extraneous motion occurs in that joint.

Arrow Grouping Low

1. Check your stance and make certain that weight is not being distributed over the foot nearest the target.

2. Adjust your bowsight downward.

3. Rotate the head toward the target and draw the string to your face without flexing your neck and moving the head toward the string.

4. Draw to your regular anchor point making certain that all facial points are contacted with the string hand; an incomplete draw will reduce arrow velocity and cause the arrows to go low on the target.

5. Check to see that you have not nocked above the ninety-degree angle.

6. Hold your anchor point until the arrow is in the target. Allowing the string to move forward—"creeping"—prior to release reduces arrow velocity.

7. Check your grip to make certain that you are not applying pressure to rotate the whole bow toward the target.

8. Maintain the correct bow-arm position without lowering it (adducting the bow-arm shoulder) until the arrow is in the target.

Archery as a sport

3

Archery may be used for recreational purposes in many ways throughout one's lifetime. Several phases of archery as a sport are described briefly in this chapter. Bow hunting and bow fishing are discussed in the following chapter.

There are three main controlling organizations for amateur archers: (1) National Archery Association, Incorporated, of the United States (NAA); (2) National Field Archery Association of the United States, Incorporated (NFAA); and (3) Federation Internationale DeTir a L'Arc—International Archery Federation (FITA).

According to the NAA constitution, "The purpose of the NAA shall be to perpetuate, foster, and direct the practice of archery in the United States in accordance with the high spirit and honorable tradition of that most ancient sport." This is accomplished by means of a variety of services to archers, and the publishing of *Archery World*. The NAA is *the* sports governing body for archery in America. The NAA has its headquarters at 2833 Lincoln Highway East, Ronks, Pennsylvania 17572.

The legalizing of bow hunting led indirectly to the development of the NFAA following World War II. This organization provides specialized field rounds more analogous to bow-hunting situations than to target rounds. Consequently, field archers can combine their target and hunting interests. NFAA headquarters are located at Route 2, Box 514, Redlands, California 92373. *Archery Magazine* is the official publication of the NFAA.

FITA was officially formed in 1931. This organization establishes rules and helps regulate world championships in archery. The NAA is affiliated with the FITA.

TARGET ARCHERY

For competitive purposes, most high school and college archers would be in one of the following four NAA classifications:

1. Men—eighteen years of age or more
2. Women—eighteen years of age or more
3. Intermediate Boys—fifteen to eighteen years of age
4. Intermediate Girls—fifteen to eighteen years of age

The NAA lists twenty-three different official rounds. Space permits only a brief discussion of the championship and a few popular rounds for archers in the above classifications.

Championship Rounds

Men's F.I.T.A. Round   The Men's F.I.T.A. Round is shot at a ten-ring scoring target face. Thirty-six arrows are shot from ninety meters (98.46 yards), seventy meters (76.58 yards), fifty meters (54.7 yards), and thirty meters (32.82 yards) respectively. This is a grand total of 144 arrows per round. The 122-centimeter, ten-ring target face is used at the two greatest distances, and the 80-centimeter, ten-ring target face is utilized at the two closest distances.

In World Class competition, two of these rounds must be shot for total score. It is not unusual for the winning archer to average close to 8.50 points per arrow. Scores of 2400 or better are considered to be excellent for the F.I.T.A. Round. To gain some appreciation of this type of feat, the beginning archer should attempt to shoot at the ten-ring, 122-centimeter target from the ninety-meter distance. Target archery can be an extremely demanding sport!

Women's F.I.T.A. Round   Women shoot 36 arrows from seventy meters (76.58 yards), sixty meters (65.64 yards), fifty meters (54.70 yards), and thirty meters (32.82 yards) respectively. This also makes a grand total of 144 arrows per round. Like the men, the women also use the 122-centimeter, ten-ring target at the two longer distances, and the 80-centimeter, ten-ring target at the two shortest distances in the round.

Women who place within the top twenty archers in the world championships usually shoot scores which exceed 1050 for each round. A woman who shoots a two-round score of 2360 would be a contender in most World Class competitions.

The 900 Round   This is an NAA championship round shot on a forty-eight-inch target face, but it is scored on a ten-point basis. The round consists of shooting ninety arrows. Thus, by using ten-ring scoring, 900 would be the perfect score for this round. Five ends are shot from sixty yards, fifty yards, and forty yards respectively. The 900 Round is for men, women, intermediate boys, and girls.

The American Round   This round is for women, men, and intermediate archers. Five ends or thirty arrows are shot from sixty, fifty, and forty yards respectively. As in any competitive target archery round, the greatest distance is shot on the first day. This number of ends amounts to a total of ninety arrows for the round and a possible perfect score of 810. An American Round score of 630 to 680 for a college student in an archery class would be considered in the "good" category. Competitive men archers shoot American Round scores consistently above the 750 point. Scores by women are above 700 for this round, and the national winner's score at the university level will exceed 700 by a comfortable margin. An archer desiring to become an intercollegiate champion in this round should plan to shoot scores that exceed 775 on a consistent basis. This type of performance would usually place the archer in a contender's category.

Nonchampionship Rounds

The following nonchampionship rounds are recognized by the NAA and are shot on the regulation forty-eight-inch target face:

YORK ROUND
72 arrows at 100 yards
48 arrows at 80 yards
24 arrows at 60 yards

COLUMBIA ROUND
24 arrows at 50 yards
24 arrows at 40 yards
24 arrows at 30 yards

JUNIOR COLUMBIA ROUND
24 arrows at 40 yards
24 arrows at 30 yards
24 arrows at 20 yards

SCHOLASTIC ROUND
24 arrows at 40 yards
24 arrows at 30 yards

TEAM ROUNDS
96 arrows at 60 yards—men
96 arrows at 50 yards—women

NATIONAL ROUND
48 arrows at 60 yards
24 arrows at 50 yards

JUNIOR AMERICAN ROUND
30 arrows at 50 yards
30 arrows at 40 yards
30 arrows at 30 yards

WESTERN ROUND
48 arrows at 60 yards
48 arrows at 50 yards

HEREFORD ROUND

72 arrows at 80 yards

48 arrows at 60 yards

24 arrows at 50 yards

WINDSOR ROUND

36 arrows at 60 yards

36 arrows at 50 yards

36 arrows at 40 yards

ALBION ROUND

36 arrows at 80 yards

36 arrows at 60 yards

36 arrows at 50 yards

SAINT GEORGE ROUND

36 arrows at 100 yards

36 arrows at 80 yards

36 arrows at 60 yards

SAINT NICHOLAS ROUND

48 arrows at 40 yards

36 arrows at 30 yards

Unique Rounds

Clout Round   The Clout Round is shot from 180 yards by men, and 140 yards by women. Thirty-six arrows are shot during the round. The target is laid out on the ground, and its outer circle measures forty-eight feet in diameter instead of the regulation forty-eight inches commonly seen in the regulation target face. The target has the standard concentric circles, but the center is marked by a white flag.

Historically, clout shooting can be traced at least as far back as the period of English archery prior to The Hundred Years' War. Clout shooting has been used in many wars throughout history. The archers shot great volleys of arrows into the air in clout fashion toward their opponents. This was an early and effective form of aerial bombardment. The reader can readily understand the apprehension of a soldier as a volley of arrows numbering in the thousands suddenly descends into his area. In addition to being an effective killing technique, the arrival of the arrows caused panic among the ranks on numerous occasions.

Wand Round   Wand shooting consists of shooting thirty-six arrows at a piece of balsa wood two inches in width projecting six feet upward from the ground. The scoring is simple, but achieving a score is extremely difficult! Any arrow embedded in the wand counts as a hit. Also, a witnessed rebound from the wand counts as a hit. The challenge of wand shooting lies in the distances involved. Men shoot at the two-inch wand from 100 yards, intermediate boys from 80 yards, and women as well as intermediate girls shoot at the wand from 60 yards. This is an extremely difficult task. Wand

---

Using the formula $s = \frac{1}{2} at^2$ (s = distance; a = gravity; t = time in seconds), how far above the target must an arrow be aimed to make nine points if you are shooting with a bow that imparts the arrow at 100 feet per second from 30 yards? with a bow that imparts the arrow at 200 feet per second?

---

shooting is referred to periodically in English literature dating back into the twelfth and thirteenth centuries.

FIELD ARCHERY

The NFAA is dedicated to bow hunting, conservation, the preservation of large and small game animals, and to the promotion of field archery games. Committees are established to perform these functions within the overall organization.

Field archers compete in three different divisions. These are for bare-bow shooters, free-style shooting, and competitive bow hunters.

The bare-bow division restricts the archer to a bow without any type of sighting device whatsoever. Furthermore, no marks or blemishes can be placed on the bow which potentially could be used as a sighting device. The archer can utilize a stabilizer, but a release aid is illegal in the bare-bow division.

The free-style division allows any type of sighting device to be attached to the bow. The archer may use a release device while shooting in the free-style division competitions.

The competitive bow-hunter division rules are similar to the bare-bow division in regard to sighting devices. They are illegal. If stabilizers are mounted on the bow, they cannot be more than twelve inches in length. Furthermore, the three-finger, traditional grip must be used. This eliminates the use of a release aid for shooting in any of the competitive bow-hunter division competitions.

The NFAA recognizes the FITA and American Rounds discussed previously in this chapter. In addition, the NFAA has five official rounds: (1) Field Round, (2) Hunter's Round, (3) Animal Round, (4) N.F.A.A. International Round, and (5) Flint Bowman Indoor Round.

A field archery course differs appreciably from a target archery course. A field course consists of fourteen targets (a unit). Two units are needed for a round. Five to ten acres are desirable for each unit, and it is recommended that two units be available for each complete field course. This eliminates the necessity of having the archers moving through the same course twice. Twenty acres of wooded hills make an ideal field archery course.

Targets and distances vary from round to round in field archery. There are official NFAA targets ranging from six to twenty-four inches in diameter. These are black and white, and the sizes and distances of the targets are prescribed by the rules for each round. In addition, animal target faces can be used. As one example, targets for the Animal Round range in size from the moose to jack rabbit. High and low scoring areas are established on all official animal targets.

The NFAA also has a very active indoor archery program for promoting archery competition throughout the entire year. The emphasis in this program is on league and tournament activities.

FLIGHT SHOOTING

Flight shooting is the sport of shooting arrows to obtain maximum distance. These events are conducted under the auspices of the NAA. Restrictions for competition are based primarily on bow weights and secondarily on age and sex classifications. Each age and sex division has an unlimited weight and foot bow class. (A foot bow has a heavy draw requiring the archer to lie on his or her back and draw the string with both hands while pushing the face of the bow with the feet. This is sometimes called pedominal shooting.)

The distances obtained by expert flight shooters with excellent flight-shooting tackle is phenomenal. It is not unusual for a distance of 500 yards to be obtained by youngsters. Distances of 700 yards are not impossible for men. A knowledge of physics and principles of biomechanics as they relate to the design and construction of the archery tackle is paramount in this sport. Key factors in flight shooting are aerodynamics of the arrow as a missile and the velocity which can be obtained once the arrow is put in flight. The flight bow is designed to project an arrow at significantly greater velocities than are possible with a recurve target archery bow. For those archers who are interested in physics in general, aerodynamics, and/or biomechanics, flight shooting is a most fascinating sport.

THE OLYMPIC GAMES

Archery was a part of the Olympic Games on a demonstration basis in 1908, 1920, and 1968. Due to the efforts of many dedicated people throughout the world during the 1960s, archery became a gold medal sport in the 1972 Olympic Games. This event, highly significant to the sport of archery, has resulted in an increased interest in target archery as an amateur sport throughout the world.

Figures 3.1 and 3.2 show some of the men and women archers who were involved in the 1908 Olympic Games. These illustrations are interesting, because they give us a chance to compare and contrast the type

Fig. 3.1.   The Fourth Olympiad of 1908 held in Shepherd's Bush Stadium in London. The men shot the York Round. The central figure in the light suit is the British gold medalist, W. Dod (From E. G. Heath, **The Grey Goose Wing).**

Fig. 3.2.   The women competitors shooting the National Round at the 1908 Olympic Games (From E. G. Heath, **The Grey Goose Wing).**

Have you investigated your local opportunities for observation and participation in archery competition?

of archery tackle which was used in World Class competition in 1908 with tackle available to archers today. The long bow is predominant in both illustrations. The use of the long bow in this type of competition today would be almost unthinkable. It is also interesting to compare and contrast the type of clothing worn by the competitors in 1908 with the type of clothing worn today. The rather erratic arrow grouping shown in figure 3.2 would not place the archer very high in contemporary competition.

One of the problems we in the United States have to cope with has been that of developing amateur archers with skill great enough to compete on an international level. Many fine archers of the past are now regarded as professionals, according to the very strict Olympic Eligibility Code. Prior to 1961, the NAA did not recognize the difference between amateur and professional archers. After that time and in anticipation of Olympic status for archery, the NAA established eligibility rules for amateurs which conform to the strict Olympic Code. This act gave impetus to the development of the Professional Archers' Association (PAA) for archers who could no longer compete with amateurs on an open basis. The PAA has its headquarters at Route 1, Box 32, Hickory Corners, Michigan 49060.

Where will the Olympic archers for the United States (and other countries) come from? Today's university students, those currently interested in archery, are good prospects. With good instruction and diligent practice, the individual reading the book in hand can develop into a potential archery champion of national and international caliber within a period of one to two years. This is not impossible if the individual has tremendous intrinsic motivation toward this type of goal. A young adult or adult with the proper attitude, interest, aptitude, and motivation could possibly earn a position on the Olympic team in archery. To represent one's country on an Olympic team is one of the highest honors an individual can obtain. It is both fitting and proper that archery, one of man's oldest sports, has finally been added to the Olympic Gold Medal Sport's agenda.

Bow hunting and fishing

4

BOW HUNTING

Hunting with the bow and arrow has developed in popularity during the past decade. One reason for this lies in the fact that game animals tend to be more numerous for the bow hunter than for the gun hunter. As examples, one may bow hunt for deer, squirrel, quail, coyote, wild boar, fox, bobcat, lion, and bear. This can usually be done in advance of the hunting seasons (gun). Each animal presents a different set of problems. Many of the same problems do not exist for the gun hunter, because a man with a powerful rifle can compensate for his lack of hunting skill by virtue of the ability of his weapon. The bow hunter does not have this type of unsportsmanlike advantage. The bow hunter must be a *hunter* in every sense of the word. This is one reason for bow hunting's increased popularity in recent years. The man who really likes the true sport of the hunt including stalking will love bow hunting.

Tackle

If the archer chooses good tackle, it can be used for most forms of archery with slight modifications. The principles for purchasing hunting tackle are almost the same as those for buying target archery tackle discussed in chapter 1. There are, however, decided differences between target archery and bow-hunting tackle. The individual who wants to participate in bow hunting exclusively should purchase tackle designed specifically for bow-hunting purposes.

Hunting Bows   A thirty-five- to forty-five-pound recurve bow like those shown in figures 4.1 and 4.2 can be used by most men for hunting purposes. (It should be noted that some states place a forty-pound limit on hunting bows.) This bow weight is sufficient to provide the force needed to kill most game animals in North America. A fifty- to seventy-pound bow would be safer, however, for use against big game such as grizzly bear. A woman

Fig. 4.1.   A takedown hunting bow (Courtesy Black Widow Bows Springfield, Missouri 65807).

interested in bow hunting should purchase a lighter bow commensurate with her strength level. Most skilled women archers of average strength can readily handle a twenty-five- to thirty-five-pound bow efficiently, and this is enough bow weight to kill the vast majority of game animals.

The length of the bow for hunting is a very important consideration. Some archers believe that a short bow length is most desirable in the hunt-

Fig. 4.2.   A composite hunting bow equipped with a quiver and sight.

ing situation. Their argument usually centers around the fact that the shorter bow is less cumbersome in heavily wooded and foliaged areas. This may be true, but how many times does a good bow hunter confine himself or herself to hunting in heavy brush? It is virtually impossible to shoot accurately under these circumstances with any length bow. The arrow will strike limbs or leaves, and as a result it will not find its mark because of deflections and loss of velocity. A good bow hunter does not linger long in heavy brush.

A more serious and negative factor in regard to the short bow is the sharp angle created for the archer against the bowstring and arrow. This angle at the nocking point tends to compress the fingers of the bowstring hand so tightly that a smooth release is very difficult when using the conventional three-finger grip. A longer bow, sixty-four to seventy inches, has longer limbs and a longer bowstring; consequently, the angle created at the nocking area at full draw is greater than the same angle for the short bow. This allows a smoother release when using the three-finger grip. Ultimately, the choice of bow length is a matter of personal preference for the bow hunter. A bow such as the one shown in figure 4.1 with a length of sixty-four inches is recommended when the draw length is twenty-eight inches. This type of hunting bow is also available in fifty-six-inch and sixty-inch models.

If the bow hunter prefers bows of from fifty-six inches to sixty-two inches in length, it is recommended that a release device be utilized. As a matter of fact, the use of a release device in bow hunting is a good idea for any length bow. A release device, such as the one shown in figure 4.3, eliminates the release with a traditional grip with the sharp bowstring angle commonly seen in short bows. It also eliminates the problem of trying to release by using finger extension with extremely cold fingers. One of the main advantages of a release device over the traditional three-finger grip is that the string goes absolutely straight at the time of release instead of being deflected inward or outward. The release device is relatively easy to use when compared to using a finger tab or shooting glove. A low anchor point using a release device is shown in figure 4.4. The second, third, and fourth fingers are placed inside the handle loop. The handle loop is adjusted so there will be some pressure on the little finger during the draw. The front strap is pushed around the string with the index finger an inch *below* the arrow. Some pressure is held on the strap against the gripper pad during the draw. The gripper pad will keep the strap from slipping while the thumb and index finger are applying the pressure during the draw. The draw is made to the position shown in figure 4.5. To release the arrow, simply release the pressure exerted on the tab by the index finger and thumb (fig. 4.6). It is not necessary to pull the hand back on release while using a release device of this

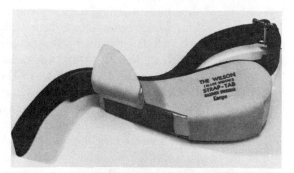

Fig. 4.3. A release device
(Courtesy Wilson Brothers).

Fig. 4.4. A low anchor point using a
release device.

Fig. 4.5. Hunting bow at full
draw using a release device.

Fig. 4.6. Release and follow-
through using a release device.

type. Many of the "human errors" are removed for the bow hunter using a release device. This is one reason release devices are no longer allowed in target archery, but they do have distinct advantages in bow-hunting situations.

A bowsight with calibrated settings for short distances of ten, twenty, thirty, and forty yards should be mounted on the hunting bow (fig. 4.2). These are the most common shooting distances in bow hunting. If you are farther than thirty to forty yards from your game animal, you are too far for a worthwhile shot! The good bow hunter will usually work for a shot from within ten to twenty-five yards of the game animal.

Some bow hunters like to make special adjustments on their bows for the hunting season. Doug Kittredge, a leading bow-hunting expert in the United States, camouflages his bow by painting it forest green. He also tapes an extra bowstring to the bow in case the one in use breaks or becomes inefficient during the hunt. It is also a good idea to attach brush buttons or string silencers to the bowstring. These are simple rubber devices which reduce the noise made by the string's vibration and slapping the face of the bow after the shot. If this type of string noise is eliminated, it may help the bow hunter get off a good second shot.

Hunting Arrows   Aluminum shafts are recommended for hunting purposes. The aluminum arrow is the most accurate on the market. Why spend considerable time and expense on a hunting trip and miss the game animal due to cheap, inaccurate arrows? The aluminum arrow can handle the heavier hunting arrow points better than fiberglass arrows. To add to arrow stability with the larger hunting point, the fletching should be lengthened to five or six inches. The arrow shaft should be white or yellow. The bright color will reduce the number of lost arrows and will not "spook" the game animal once the arrow is in flight. The hunting arrows should be matched in all respects with each other and with the hunting bow being used.

Before proceeding with a discussion of modern arrow points, let us regress somewhat and evaluate the bow-hunting tackle of the American Indian. Obviously, these people were highly successful as hunters. Their survival over hundreds of years in primitive territory testifies to their skill. Hunger tends to be a greater motivating factor for developing archery skill than a grade within a university archery class!

The Navajo Indian drawing his bow in figure 4.7 would have had considerably less trouble obtaining his game if he and his fellow hunters had had bows similar to those in figures 4.1 and 4.2, and arrow points similar to those in figure 4.9. Actually, the Navajo Indians and others developed very effective composite bows made with a backing of layers of sinew. The arrow points utilized by American Indians differ appreciably from those utilized by contemporary bow hunters. If the reader takes time to compare

Fig. 4.7. A Navajo Indian and his bow hunting tackle (From E. G. Heath. **The Grey Goose Wing**).

and contrast figures 4.8 and 4.9, these differences will become immediately apparent. Figure 4.8 shows a variety of Indian arrow and spear points which were found in the northeastern part of Missouri. Most individuals would assume that all of the points shown in figure 4.8 are arrow heads. This would be an erroneous assumption. The point on the extreme right in the picture and the point on the extreme right of the upper row are both spear points. The large, 4¾-inch long "beaver tail" point on the right side of the picture was used on a shaft of a spear. The upper right point is also a smaller, 3¼-inch-long spear point. The remaining are arrow points ranging in length from ¾ inch to 3 inches. These were actually attached to the ends of wooden arrow shafts. The small, ¾-inch-long arrow point in the lower row on the left side, is called a bird point. One theory about bird points

Fig. 4.8. Indian arrow and spear points from the collection of Loyd Howell, Wyaconda, Missouri.

indicates that they were made and used by smaller children who utilized them with light pulling bows and shot them at birds. In other words, they were considered to be functional toys used by Indian children. The unnotched arrow in the upper row is a war point. These arrows were shot into enemies. When the shaft was pulled, the arrow point remained within the body of the individual who was shot. Obviously, this posed serious ramifications in terms of removal, compounded by the perils of infections which could be lethal if the penetration by the arrow itself failed to kill the individual who was hit. This particular war point is 2½ inches in length.

Contemporary arrow points for hunting are designed to kill game by two techniques: (1) hemorrhage and (2) impact. Arrow points or broadheads designed to kill by hemorrhage *must be razor sharp* to be most effective (fig. 4.9). It is important to remember that an arrow point will not always kill an animal, because the blood vessels will not be lacerated to the extent of allowing a steady, unobstructed blood flow. The dull arrow point will tear tissue instead of cutting. A torn vein will constrict to act as its own protective mechanism against hemorrhage. The bow hunter who is attempting to kill does not want this to occur. The animal struck in this fashion will have a tendency to continue moving great distances and become lost to the hunter. The American Indian had this problem while bow hunting with the type of tackle shown in figures 4.7 and 4.8. Unlike the contemporary bow hunter, the American Indian was probably better at trailing and finding the stricken animal. An archer shooting a dull arrow must strike a

Fig. 4.9. Three different types of broadheads.

vital organ most of the time to kill the game animal, but this is not necessarily true if a razor-sharp arrow is used. Such a hit in a large muscle group, for example, will clearly sever arteries, veins, capillaries, and other blood vessels in the area. This will cause hemorrhage sufficient and fast enough to result in death rather quickly. The bow hunter merely follows the trail of blood from the stricken animal until it collapses from asphyxiation. Most large animals are taken with the bow and arrow by using the hemorrhage technique.

There are many field archers who are also interested in bow hunting. Figure 4.10 shows the type of arrow attachment which allows the archer to utilize both field points and broadheads. The field points are simply screwed into the arrow shaft when they are desired for use in field archery. They can be removed quickly and replaced with a broadhead as shown. The impact technique for killing game animals is used in bow hunting on small animals such as squirrel and rabbit. Rubber and metal blunt arrow points are shown in figure 4.11. The shock of the blunted arrow is usually enough to cause death instantaneously on the small game animals. The extreme arrow velocity imparted by the higher bow weights virtually insures the effectiveness of the impact technique while using blunts.

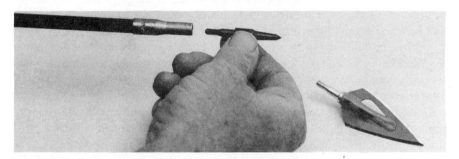

Fig. 4.10.   Interchangeable arrow for broadhead and field point use.

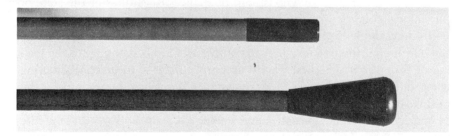

Fig. 4.11.   Blunt hunting points.

Techniques

The bow hunter needs to train and condition prior to the hunting season in order to perfect accuracy and improve upon physiologic fitness in the areas of cardiovascular endurance, muscular endurance, and strength.

Prior to the start of the hunting season, target practice is absolutely essential. If the archer has been shooting with target or field points, a switch should be made to the heavier broad heads or hunting points for preseason target practice. Flight trajectories of arrows equipped with broad heads differ considerably from trajectories of arrows equipped with target or field points. During this preseason target practice, bowsight adjustments for hunting distances will have to be made. Traditionally, these are the shorter distances of ten, fifteen, twenty, twenty-five, and thirty yards.

All shots made in the field will not be like shots on the target range; consequently, it is a good idea to practice periodically before the bow-hunting season starts on a field archery range. The good bow hunter practices on both target and field archery ranges by taking shots while in unusual positions. One should practice shooting from the knees, standing on the side of a hill, and in a variety of body positions. Also, considerable shooting should be done with the bow held at various angles ranging from vertical to horizontal. In most situations the terrain on which the actual hunting shot will be made is very difficult to predict.

Muscles will have to be strengthened and developed for the endurance required by bow hunting, especially if the hunter has been sedentary for several weeks or months prior to the opening of the bow season. When a hunter enters the field for big game animals in particular this may involve walking for miles over uneven terrain, in hills, or mountains at high elevations. Consequently, a good level of strength and muscular endurance in those muscles discussed in chapter 7 is absolutely essential. Shooting a bow and arrow when fatigued is vastly different from shooting when rested. It is entirely possible that the bow hunter may get the best shot of the year while very tired. The conditioned hunter can handle this situation much better than the individual who is "out of shape." Regardless of the state of physiologic condition of the bow hunter, anyone can become tired while performing the type of work one must do while in the field. Consequently, the bow hunter should know how to compensate in his shooting for the feeling of being tired. The best way to accomplish this is to practice shooting when fatigued as well as in the rested state. Many bow hunters make the mistake of never practicing while tired. This type of illogical practice would be analogous to a football coach never having his team work out and execute their skills while feeling the stress of competition and prolonged neuromus-

Why is it important to use hunting points during preseason target practice? How should the hunting bowsight be adjusted for such practice?

cular activity. Such a team would find the going very rough in the last few
minutes of the fourth quarter of a football game. The archer who has never
experienced shooting while fatigued would also be hard pressed to kill a
game animal if the situation presented itself in the field when he or she was
extremely tired.

Another part of the conditioning process should be directly related to
the development of cardiovascular endurance. It is recommended that the
bow hunter pursue a daily and vigorous workout schedule throughout the
entire year. To prepare the bow hunter for the walking done in conjunction with hunting, it is recommended that the bow hunter gradually increase walking or jogging distances daily prior to the hunting season. With
a man or woman going into rugged, mountainous terrain, merely walking
throughout the entire year is inadequate for conditioning purposes. Regular
jogging is recommended for development of cardiovascular endurance. A
recommended procedure would be to first obtain your annual checkup from
the family physician including a working electrocardiogram. If the physician
determines that you are in a state of good cardiovascular health, a walking-
jogging program should be started on a daily basis. It is recommended that
this should be for a minimum of twenty to thirty minutes daily. The walking-jogging rate should be fast enough to elevate the pulse rate into a range
of 130-150 beats per minute. This type of routine should be followed
throughout the year. For one month prior to the bow-hunting season, the
walking-jogging workout would be followed by an hour of shooting at some
type of target with arrows fully equipped with broad heads. If this type of
training program is followed, no terrain will be too difficult for the bow
hunter. It will take much longer for fatigue to develop. And, if fatigue does
develop, shooting will be no problem.

The bow hunter should practice judging distances constantly throughout the year. This can be done almost anywhere. As an example, while
walking pick out a sign, tree, person, or object and estimate its distance.
When this has been done, count your steps as you move toward the object
selected. Judgment of distance will improve steadily through such practice.
Why is this important to the bow hunter? If a bowsight is used as recommended, it will help gauge distances more precisely when in the hunting
environment. Thus, the bowsight setting can be more accurate and this can
lead to more game.

Like the Indian of yesteryear, the bow hunter must become very familiar with the game being sought. Eating and drinking habits must be known, and the bow hunter must be very familiar with the habitat of the animals being pursued. It is a good idea to go into the hunting area on foot a few weeks prior to the hunting season to study or scout intended game. As an example, a deer herd may be observed for several days. Their eating, drinking, and bedding habits can be observed if the individual is an excellent hunter. Some people are so good at this that they actually choose the deer to be shot prior to the opening day of the season. This takes considerable patience, knowledge, and hunting skill. Many hunters of the "instant hunting school" are in such a hurry to kill their game animals that they fail to enjoy the hunt. One misses a great deal while driving on back country roads in a pickup truck or on a motorcycle looking for wild game!

An important part of any hunt is the fine art of stalking or seeking out game animals. This is more important in bow hunting than gun hunting, because the bow hunter must get closer to the game animal to make the kill. Most deer, for example, are killed with the bow and arrow at distances ranging from ten to forty yards. The gun hunter, on the other hand, will kill deer with high-powered rifles at distances of up to one hundred yards or more. The good bow hunter shoots the deer while the deer is in a non-moving position. To obtain that type of shot, the bow hunter must be an excellent stalker with an intimate knowledge of both the deer and the environment. In addition, such factors as habits of the animal, common noises and scents in the area, wind direction changes by time of day, animal camouflage techniques, and animal movements must be thoroughly understood by the bow hunter.

The bow hunter must also face one fact prior to stalking game animals. Regardless of cleanliness, the human body has odors atypical to those in the hunting area. These odors come from skin, breath, hair, and human habits such as the use of tobacco and liquor. If the hunter does not hunt into the air currents, he is in real trouble. Every animal will know that a predator, man in this case, is in the area. The hunter should try to eliminate all odors of civilization. This can be accomplished, in part, through a study of wind patterns. Wind patterns differ depending upon the time of day and nature of the terrain. These should be studied, preferably prior to the opening of bow-hunting season. If this is not possible, it will take some very astute observations on the part of the bow hunter to study these patterns while in the process of hunting. Odors from the hunter should be eliminated by using pine-scented soap, and refraining from the use of tobacco and liquor while on the hunt.

There is a great sport associated with bow hunting which actually depends upon specialized noise. This sport is known as *varmint calling*. This is a sport utilizing noise to attract predatory animals. The predator hears the noise made by the hunter thinking it is an animal in distress. The game animal becomes the stalker, and the bow hunter actually becomes the hunted object. This can be very exciting, especially when the predator is in the big cat family!

The varmint caller uses a hand-built or commercially built device to attract the predator. The sound of the call is not like any emitted by any particular animal; however, it does resemble the squeal of many animals in distress. This noise attracts the predator, because he associates the crying sound with previous experiences while on a hunt. The motivating drive for the game animal is hunger. When the predator gets within a few feet of the area where the bow hunter is camouflaged, the hunter releases the arrow (fig. 4.12). The distance of the shot depends largely upon the hunter's courage and skill. Animal calls work very effectively on the carnivorous predatory animals, but they are relatively ineffective on such animals as deer and elk.

Noise can be used in many situations to the bow hunter's advantage. Many hunters believe that they should be absolutely quiet at all times on the hunt. It is virtually impossible to be quiet in all hunting situations. Noise that is not typical of the environment should be avoided as much as possible when stalking. However, noise can be used to flush game out of thick, brushy areas where a shot would be very unwise. This usually panics the animals and causes them to move rapidly in several directions. A shot

Fig. 4.12. Camouflaged bow hunter (Courtesy Bow and Arrow Magazine).

while the animals are moving would most likely be wasted. Noise can be used, however, to flush birds from their hiding places in high grass or brushy areas. This is common practice in hunting birds such as quails and pheasant with the bow and arrow (fig. 4.13). Hitting a bird on the wing with an arrow is a real challenge!

Excessive talking and noises associated with human beings should be avoided as much as possible. A broken twig may alarm an animal, but animals in a wooded area are familiar with such noises. They usually respond by looking intently in the direction of the sound. The best thing to do following such a noise is to remain motionless for a few minutes. A grazing animal who has heard such a sound will return to eating after assuring himself that a predator is not stalking in the immediate area.

It may seem obvious, but the bow hunter must know how to see the animal being sought. This takes considerable practice and experience. In their natural habitat, animals are capable of hiding or camouflaging themselves very effectively. The untrained eye can miss seeing a potential shot. Some animals, especially birds such as pheasant and quail, depend upon their cover and camouflage for protection even more than on their movement abilities. There are no secrets for spotting game animals. The bow hunter should know the coloring of the animal being sought and how these colors change with the seasons. And, the bow hunter should know how the colors blend with the foliage in the environment where the hunt will take place. Anytime a bow hunter walks through a forest or wooded area, it helps

Fig. 4.13. Bird hunting (Courtesy Bow and Arrow Magazine).

to practice on this skill by trying to observe every detail in the area. This practice will help develop visual acuity or awareness.

For the individual who likes to hunt, bow hunting can occupy many leisure hours. The game animals can be as small as quail or as large as an elephant. The environment can range from the wilderness areas of Canada to the deserts of the Southwest. Bow hunting is for the adventurous individual who respects nature, sport, conservation principles, and himself as a sportsman.

BOW FISHING

Bow fishing is growing in popularity in several states. Special tackle is required if the archer wants to try this particular sport. Fishing arrow points are designed in many shapes and forms. A typical bow-fishing arrow point is shown in figures 4.14, 4.15, and 4.16. It can be seen that this type of arrow point is relatively heavy, especially when compared to the target point. The fishing arrow comes equipped with a form of barbs which help to gaff the fish once the fish has been penetrated by the arrow. As shown in figure 4.16,

Fig. 4.14.   Bow fishing point in position to be shot.

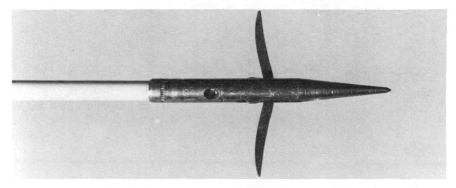

Fig. 4.15.   Bow fishing point open to gaff the fish.

Fig. 4.16.   Bow fishing point adjustment which allows it to be pulled from the fish.

this particular arrowhead is easily removed from the fish. The arrow shaft simply unscrews and allows the barb to move forward so the arrow can be removed easily from the fish once it is safely in the boat, creel, or on land. Bow-fishing arrow shafts are relatively heavy because they are made of solid plastic. They do not need the precise workmanship required for target or field archery arrows. No fletching is required on these arrows, but many do come equipped with small, rubber fletching. The arrow must be relatively heavy because it does travel through water for some distance prior to hitting the fish. Not all fish accommodate the archer by swimming on top of the water. Bow-fishing reels on the market are designed to satisfy any individual preference. They range from hand winding designs to ultra-automatic reels. A simple bow-fishing reel is shown mounted on the back of the bow in figure 4.17.

Fig. 4.17. Bow fishing (Courtesy of Bow and Arrow Magazine).

Bow fishing can be more challenging than any other form of archery. The difficulties of conquering the basic fundamentals of bow fishing are compounded by the water and other natural forces. Let us consider the plight of a bow fisherman in a boat on a river such as the situation shown in figure 4.17. If the wind is mild, and the water is disturbed slightly, the boat would be rocking as the game fish is sighted. First, the archer must stand in the boat to position himself for the shot. One of the major problems commences as he tries to aim while weaving from side to side to maintain his own upright position in the boat. In addition, the archer finds that shooting at fish is different from shooting at a land target. The land target does not have water in front of it to distort the view. The archer, therefore, must calculate the refraction of the sun's light rays as they penetrate the water in the immediate area of the game fish. This is further complicated by the fact that the actual depth of the fish is deceptive to the naked eye. The light rays from the sun have a tendency to bend downward. The archer must aim at an area in front of the fish if he is to have any chance of hitting it. Another frustrating factor is the fact that fish simply will not hold still for any appreciable length of time to allow an archer to aim for a good shot. The bow fisherman does have problems. *These problems are what make bow fishing a sport.* The bow fisherman can derive considerable personal satisfaction when these problems are overcome and the fish is landed.

States have different laws regarding bow fishing. Bow fishing and spear fishing are usually placed in the same category when legislative action is considered. The bow fisherman, like the bow hunter, must check local fish and game laws for specifics regarding bow-fishing and bow-hunting regulations. These laws change periodically; consequently, they should be read on an annual basis. Generally, however, such fish as carp, gar, and catfish can be taken with bow and arrow in most states. Ocean fishing sometimes requires a professional fishing license for the bow fisherman.

The evolution of archery

5

The history of archery and its significance to mankind, if known completely, would fill an encyclopedia. A few selected historical events are outlined within this chapter to help place archery's history in some perspective for the reader.

Archery skill was of vital importance for the survival of mankind for thousands of years. In this respect, archery played a prominent role in the growth and development of individuals, societies, and nations. Archery may have been as important in this respect as the development of the wheel, fire, and speech. Ancient man certainly learned how to use the bow and arrow effectively. If today's student had to depend upon archery skill for personal protection and securing food, the skill level would be dramatically accelerated.

Primitive artists drew bow hunters in caves located in Spain and Southern France. Ancient sculptors carved archer warriors in Egypt to honor them for their feats. The bow is known to have been used by primitive tribes throughout the world as a musical instrument. Many theologians believed that David's biblical harp was his bow. The bow can be plucked much like the bass fiddle and the harp.

Archery feats have given rise to many myths throughout history. The mythology of Greece, as one example, includes archery feats by such famed characters as Apollo, Diana, Hercules, and Eros. The English had their Robin Hood, and ancient cultures in the Far East had their heroes who were analogous to Robin Hood.

Archery has been used as an integral aspect of religious ceremonies by numerous sects in the past. The Assyrians concluded a religious ritual by shooting an arrow toward the sun. It is interesting to note that this same type of ritual, the sun vow, was practiced by Indians on the southwest plains of America many centuries later.

The Zen Buddhists place great value on archery. The Zen sect does not recognize any dichotomy between the so-called "mind" and "body." Their philosophy includes the concept that various exercises of the body, including archery, can bring the practitioner into a state of one complete being. There are times when Buddhists hold the bow at full draw for many hours until they feel the unification between "mind" and "soul." At that time, *Satori* is reached. The archer is no longer conscious of himself or the target and the arrow is released. Figure 5.1 shows Eugen Herrigel, the author of *Zen in the Art of Archery*, who was one of the few non-Orientals accepted to study the Way of Archery within the Zen Buddhist philosophy. His book is considered to be a classic in this area. The reader should compare and contrast his stance and nonexistent anchor point with figure 2.18. The draw without an anchor is typical among Zen archers.

Man's ability to use the bow and arrow to his advantage has changed the course of history on several occasions. Let us look at a few of these events chronologically.

Fig. 5.1. A rare photograph of the late Eugen Herrigel, author of **Zen in the Art of Archery** (From E. G. Heath, **The Grey Goose Wing).**

UPPER PALEOLITHIC PERIOD

It is virtually impossible to historically document that time in prehistory when man started using bows and arrows. From artifacts such as arrow points and tools believed to have been used in making tackle, it is generally agreed that man started using crude archery tackle at a time during the Upper Paleolithic period, or ten thousand to twenty thousand years ago.

Drawings in caves believed to have been inhabited by Cro-Magnon man, depict archers hunting for wild game with fairly sophisticated bows and arrows. It is logical, therefore, to assume that archery tackle must have been in use many centuries prior to the time of Cro-Magnon man. The results of carbon testing techniques applied to stone artifacts tend to give credence to this assumption. Figure 5.2 shows a Mesolithic hunting scene from a rock painting at Los Caballos, Valltorta, Spain. It is interesting to note the various types of bows carried by the archers, and the fact that the archers are depicted as being very accurate.

Fig. 5.2. Mesolithic hunting scene from a rock painting at Los Caballos, Valltorta, Spain (From E. G. Heath, **The Grey Goose Wing).**

Bows of any great age have not been found, because wood deteriorates rapidly. The oldest extant bows date back to about 1000 B.C. These were found in the Nile River valley—a very dry climate. Some museums in America have bows made by Indians of the Southwest or arid region of the United States, but these date back no more than two to three hundred years.

HOLOCENE PERIOD

5000 B.C.

The Egyptians were able to free themselves from the Persians during this age. They became superior archers through diligent practice, and this proved to be most important in battle. Spears, sling shots, and slings probably were the primary weapons of war prior to the refinement of the bow and arrow and archery skill by the Egyptians during this time in history.

1000 B.C.

The Persians moved to the area north and east of the Black and Caspian Seas to battle the Scythians. Each army had trained archers as foot soldiers, but the mounted archers of the Persians proved to be too much for the Scythians. This utilization of mounted archers added another dimension to the use of archery skills during time of war—a technique that was applied time and again by other military leaders for several centuries.

A.D. 850-950

There are records which indicate that during this hundred-year period, the Vikings helped design a new procedure for the use of the bow and arrow in time of war. It appears that prior to some amphibious assaults, their archers launched great clouts or volleys of arrows into their intended target area. This was an early form of naval bombardment. Naval bombardment of a more sophisticated nature was used extensively in World War II, the Korean War, and to a limited extent in the Vietnam War.

A.D. 1066

The Norman archers taught the English a long-lasting lesson at the Battle of Hastings (fig. 5.3). The Normans planned and executed a false retreat maneuver designed to draw the English archers out of their hiding places to pursue what seemed to them to be fleeing Normans. When the English made their move into the open, they were attacked by the enemy, and slaughtered. In this particular situation, the English were the superior archers and probably would have won the Battle of Hastings if the false retreat by the Normans had not been successful. This lesson was not wasted on the English, because they used the same kind of tactics on the French some three hundred years later at the Battle of Poitier.

A famous tapestry, the Bayeux Tapestry, was embroidered by the women friends and relatives of the English archers who fought at the Battle of Hastings (fig. 5.4). This tapestry is a band of linen 20 inches wide and 231 feet long. Various aspects of the Battle of Hastings are portrayed on the tapestry. One segment shows clearly that King Harold was hacked to death by Norman horseman instead of dying as a result of an arrow wound in the eye as erroneously recorded by some historians. Figure 5.4 shows Nor-

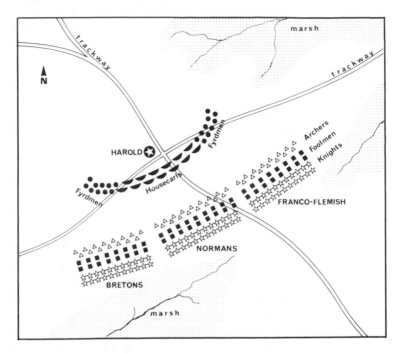

Fig. 5.3. The Battle of Hastings showing the positions of the Saxon and Norman armies at 9:00 a.m. on the 14th of October, 1066 (From E. G. Heath, **The Grey Goose Wing).**

Fig. 5.4. A portion of The Bayeux Tapestry (From E. G. Heath, **The Grey Goose Wing).**

man archers carrying short bows and drawing them to their rib cage in order to obtain maximum range. The type of bow shown is very inefficient from a physics standpoint, especially when compared to contemporary bows. Actually, the bows shown in the Bayeux Tapestry are believed to be closer to the Saxon pattern than to the longer Norman version. One explanation of this lies in the fact that the women who embroidered this tapestry were not bow experts.

A.D. 1220

Like the Persians, Genghis Khan, placed his soldiers/archers on horseback. This "Golden Horde" had great mobility and disrespect for human life, factors which allowed Genghis Khan to capture territory from the Pacific Ocean to the Volga River, and from the Caspian Sea to Northern

Fig. 5.5.   Mounted Samaurai Warrior of Japan wore plated armor as protection, horned helmet, and a guard cover over the back. (Courtesy Bow and Arrow Magazine).

Siberia. The Japanese also used mounted samurai warriors effectively (fig. 5.5). In order to obtain some insight into the accuracy difficulties encountered by the mounted archer, it is recommended that the reader try nocking, drawing, and shooting an arrow while mounted on a galloping horse.

A.D. 1252

It was during this period in English history that the long bow was established as the national weapon of England. This is a surprising fact, because recurve bow designs were well known to the English bowyers. Various types of recurve bows had been used for centuries, and portrayed in various works of art. As one example, there is a series of statues dated 490-80 B.C., from the Temple of Aigina, which depict archers using highly sophisticated recurve bows. Since this design is superior from a physics standpoint, why did the English choose the long bow as their national weapon? One possible explanation lies in the fact that the recurve bow must be made of a composite of materials glued together. England is a damp country, and the crude glue used at that time was not durable. Consequently, a composite bow might well fall apart when put to use by archers. This type of malfunction on the part of the bow would have been very embarrassing and fatal in the midst of battle. The long bow, although not as efficient as the recurve bow, was more reliable for the English under the circumstances.

A.D. 1340-63

This period marked the start of the rise of English archery superiority. The Hundred Years' War was getting under way with France. The first of the big encounters was the Battle of Crecy in A.D. 1346 (fig. 5.6). Edward III, King of England, had thirteen thousand archers at his disposal plus three thousand knights and men-at-arms who were deployed in three divisions. It is interesting to note that a teenager, the sixteen-year-old Prince of Wales (The Black Prince), was the commander of one of these divisions. The English used their archers in wedge formations. This tactic plus their supe-

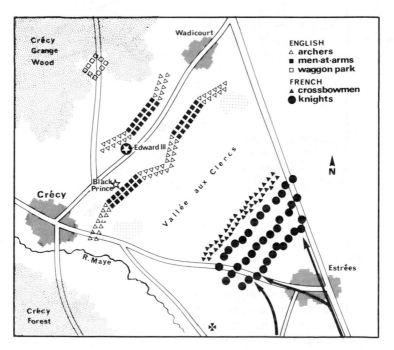

Fig. 5.6. The Battle of Crecy, August 26, 1346 (From E. G. Heath, **The Grey Goose Wing**).

Fig. 5.7. The Battle of Poitiers, 1356 (From E. G. Heath, **The Grey Goose Wing).**

rior skill with the bow and arrow enabled them to slaughter the majority of the French archers. The French force, numbering approximately forty thousand, was soundly beaten. To recognize the efforts of some of his knights in this battle, Edward III established the famous Most Noble Order of the Garter.

It was during this time period that Edward declared that archery had to be practiced by the people, and that all other sports would be illegal. This dictate by the king had a direct effect on the level of archery skill for the entire population. It is interesting to note that this type of national legislative action would be analogous to having President Franklin D. Roosevelt passing a law during World War II requiring every American to practice daily with the military rifle. While Edward III's edict had some positive ramifications for England, it is most likely that a democratic society would frown on that type of legislation.

The Battle of Poitier took place in A.D. 1356 (fig. 5.7). The English warriors were now under the command of the Black Prince. At this battle, they were outnumbered more than two to one, but were able to conquer the French. They did this by drawing the French into the open using a false retreat technique similar to that employed against them by the Normans three hundred years earlier. The French were literally killed by the thousands. The horses were the special targets in this particular battle. When the horses were wounded, the riders were unable to control them, which added to the chaos.

A.D. 1414

The Battle of Agincourt was the last big battle won by English archers. The English were outnumbered by the French four to one, but King Henry V was able to conquer the French mainly by superior archery ability on the part of the English. Shakespeare wrote of the casualties of this battle in his *King Henry V*. He indicated that twenty-nine English were slain as opposed to ten thousand French archers. The critical day of the Battle of Agincourt is shown in figure 5.9.

Fig. 5.8. An archer of 1400 A.D. from a design, originally produced for a rifle shooting trophy, by Benjamin Wyon the medallist. This is now the emblem for the Grand National Archery Society of England. (From E. G. Heath, **The Grey Goose Wing).**

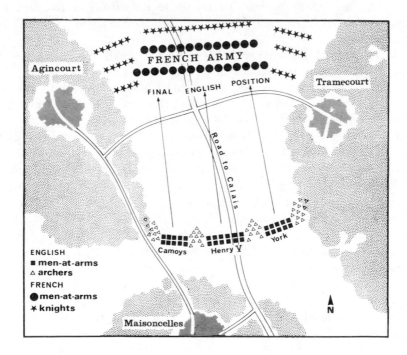

Fig. 5.9. The Battle of Agincourt, October 25, 1415. Note how the space narrows between the two forests of Agincourt and Tramecourt, which hampered any forward action by the French (From E. G. Heath, **The Grey Goose Wing).**

A.D. 1453

This time period marked the end of the Hundred Years' War. The fact that the English archers were superior to the French is historically significant both to those countries and to America as we know it. What if the French had won the Hundred Years' War? There probably would have been an entirely different series of events following the fifteenth century. The sixteenth century was marked by religious and social uheaval in England, which helped bring about the subsequent exploratory migrations to America by various English populations. It is doubtful whether the same volume of migration from England would have materialized had the French won that war. America would have been settled undoubtedly, but the political, social, and religious structures of this country might have been entirely different. The edict of Edward III requiring all Englishmen to practice archery did in fact shape history, especially American history!

A.D. 1455-71

The Wars of the Roses came about as a result of the feudal power displayed by some English lords who had acquired their strength during the preceding century. Professional military archers returning from France were hired by

Fig. 5.10.   Archers of Edward IV (1442-1483). The archers in military costume are using the yew longbow and carry twenty-four arrows (From E. G. Heath, **The Grey Goose Wing**).

these nobles for the purpose of solidifying their place in the structure of the nobility. Generally, the soldiers did a poor job simply because they lacked both military leadership and the discipline they had known previously. The last battle during the Wars of the Roses was at Tewkesbury. The significance of archery as a weapon of war was still promiment, but firearms were beginning to be used, and were more of a factor, during this period.

A.D. 1545

Roger Ascham published his book, *The Schole of Shootynge*. This was the first book ever written in the English language about archery tackle and techniques. This classic archery textbook was also published later under the title of *Toxophilus*.

A.D. 1588

The English and Spanish used firearms rather extensively at the invasion of the Spanish Armada. Most historians use this battle to denote the decline of archery as a weapon of war, but archers were nevertheless used on a smaller scale in battles for the next two hundred years.

A.D. 1917-73

During World War I, World War II, the Korean War, and Vietnam War, bows and arrows were used on a very limited basis. This seems somewhat preposterous in the "atomic age," but it is true. Some military missions call for killing people very quiety. There are not too many ways to do this, especially from a distance. Expert archers have been trained in the military for sniper duties, reconnaissance work, and sabotage. Special arrows are made for demolition work and killing by hemorrhage. Marines train men for this type of activity in their reconnaissance companies, and the Army trains special ranger groups in many of the ancient arts of killing human beings silently. Archery is one of these potential techniques.

Although somewhat outdated in terms of more sophisticated killing techniques, it must be remembered that an arrow is a very effective killing instrument whether it be for a game animal or another human being. An arrow at short range has greater penetrating potential, for example, than a .45 caliber bullet shot from a pistol. Furthermore, a skilled military archer on a reconnaissance mission has a better chance of surviving that mission than a soldier who kills with a noisy pistol. This is one reason archery was used during this period.

It is hoped that archery will never again be utilized for killing human beings in war. During the last quarter of the twentieth century, archery is used extensively as a sport. This is the best single use for bows and arrows!

Archery in literature and art

6

The bow and arrow has been a part of man's tools since the Upper Paleolithic period; consequently, it is not surprising to find references made to archery feats in the literature and art of mankind throughout history. This chapter is concerned with selected references to literary works and works of art wherein the authors or artists have referred to archery feats or archers. The student taking college archery as a general education or liberal arts subject is encouraged to look for further literature and art where archery is involved. This is another way in which physical education can contribute to the liberal arts education of the college student.

LITERATURE

There is considerable mythology surrounding the constellation Sagittarius. Sagittarius is a large southern constellation which the Greeks called a centaur. The centaur was supposed to be shooting an arrow. The term "sagittarius" actually means *the archer*. Sagittarius is located south of Aquila, and is partly in the Milky Way. It is east of Antares, one of the central stars in the constellation known as Scorpio. Sagittarius can be seen during the months of August and September in the United States. Figure 6.1 shows a schematic diagram of Sagittarius.

The various stars within Sagittarius form parts of the archer and his bow and arrow. Rukbat is the archer's knee; Arkab is the archer's tendon; Ascella is the archer's armpit or axillary region; Media is the midpoint of the bow; and Al Nasl is the arrow point. As the reader will note in figure 6.1;

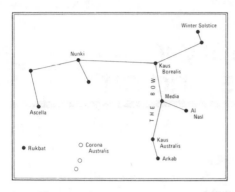

Fig. 6.1   Sagittarius

it took a vivid imagination to visualize an archer amidst that celestial configuration.

Greek mythological literature called the centaur of Sagittarius Chiron. Chiron was the famous son of Philyra and Saturn. Ovid noted that Chiron was slain by Hercules with a poisoned arrow. Jupiter, the Father of the Gods, was responsible for placing Chiron among the constellations. Ovid wrote: "Midst Golden Stars he stands refulgent now and thrusts the Scorpian with his bended bow." The reference is to the relationship between Al Nasl and Antares.

In mythological literature Apollo was the God of Archery, among other things. He was credited with numerous extraordinary feats with the bow and arrow. One of the most famous of these mythologic events was related to have taken place on Mount Parnassus. A great python was raiding families who lived in the area. The python smashed homes and ate human beings as if there were no end. Apollo decided to put a stop to all of that, so he took his bow and arrows in pursuit of the python. He ultimately found the python and invited him to fight. As is the case in most myths, good triumphed over evil. Apollo fought the python for four hours and finally killed him with an accurately placed arrow.

Shortly following the battle with the python, Apollo encountered Eros, or Cupid. He insulted Eros by telling him that a boy should not play with a man's weapons. The reference, of course, was to the bow and arrows carried by Eros. This act by Apollo enraged Eros. He decided to get even with Apollo. This he did by shooting Apollo with a golden arrow of love. Apollo immediately fell in love with Daphne. Daphne was the daughter of Peneun, the River God. Eros promptly shot Daphne with a lead arrow of hate. Daphne's feeling for Apollo was one of disgust. Ultimately, she turned herself into a laurel tree. Apollo, in love with Daphne to the end, showed his undying love by hanging his bow and quiver on her limbs.

Eros had many adventures in mythological literature with his bow and arrow. The term "eros" is rather interesting. It serves as the root word for the term "erotic" which coincides with the purpose of the existence of Eros. The term "eros" also gave rise to the term "arrows."

One of the greatest mythological archers was Hercules, or Herakles. Hercules is better known for his feats of strength, but he was also responsible for many remarkable accomplishments with the bow and arrow. For example, he was primarily responsible for the conquest of Troy due to his prowess with the bow and arrow. Hercules killed Paris with one of his arrows during the Trojan War. Earlier, it will be remembered that Paris had shot Achilles with a poisoned arrow. That was described as a remarkable archery shot, because the Achilles heel area was the only vulnerable area on the body of Achilles. Anatomists refer to the tendon from the gastrocnemius and soleus muscles to the calcaneus bone as "the Achilles tendon."

There is another minor constellation known as Sagitta the Arrow. This constellation is located in the Milky Way just north of the constellation known as the Eagle. In comparing and discussing Sagittarius and Sagitta, Aratos wrote, "There further shot another arrow but this with a bow. Towards it the Bird more northward flies." The references are to Sagittarius and the Eagle. Eratosthenes considered Sagitta to be the shaft with which Apollo exterminated the Cyclops. It was also referred to as one of Cupid's arrows in mythological literature.

Fig. 6.2. The Education of Achilles by Chiron (From E. G. Heath, **The Grey Goose Wing**).

Fig. 6.3.   Odysseus, on returning home from his many wanderings slays the suitors of Penelope, his wife. The use of a thumb release can be assumed due to the position of his bowstring hand—Fifth Century B.C. (From E. G. Heath, **The Grey Goose Wing**).

As we move forward historically, other characters bordering on the mythological emerged in the literature. Robin Hood fits into this category. There is no strong evidence to support the fact that such a person actually lived. It is possible, however. As his legend grew, the truth about his feats with the bow and arrow could have been distorted. This is a common characteristic of mythology, i.e., one is apt to find historically substantiated subject matter combined with feats and episodes purely mythological in nature.

There is a legendary report of a wand shoot between Robin Hood and Clifton. According to the tale, Clifton shot his arrow first and hit the two-inch wand at one hundred yards. Before Clifton's arrow stopped oscillating, Robin Hood released his arrow and completely split the shaft of Clifton's vibrating arrow The mathematical probability of the occurrence of such an event is fantastic. Even with modern tackle, it is highly improbable that such a feat could occur. The best contemporary trick shot archers usually make their shots at distances of ten to twenty yards. Some movie stunt men do not rely on skill alone for close-up shots of arrows penetrating a human body. To do this the arrow is mounted on wire and guided directly to its mark where it penetrates a large pad strategically placed under the stunt man's clothing. Such procedures by contemporary professional archers make the story of Robin Hood's wand shot even more fantastic.

There is a grave in England supposedly occupied by Robin Hood. A portion of the epitaph reads, ". . . No archer was like him so good; his wild-

Fig. 6.4. An eighteenth century engraving of Robin Hood by Thomas Bewick (From E. G. Heath, **The Grey Goose Wing**).

ness named him Robin Hood." (His real name was supposed to be Robert, Earl of Huntington.) It is rather interesting that the vernacular term for someone who lives an obstreperous life outside the law is "hood."

Schiller, the famed German poet and dramatist, wrote a play featuring a very dramatic arrow shot. This was *Wilhelm Tell*. The tale centered around a Swiss archer who had the courage and archery skill to defy an invading regime. The archer was able to demonstrate his skill by shooting through an apple sitting on his son's head. A shot like Tell's in real life would have been remarkable, because the father had to shoot at his son in a stress situation with poorly constructed archery tackle. The student of archery and literature may want to try to duplicate some of the legendary archery feats found within the literature. This is recommended, especially to check on their validity. In the case of the shot by Wilhelm Tell, however, it would be wise to use an apple sitting on a balloon for obvious reasons.

James Fenimore Cooper wrote many portrayals of the American Indian. There are many factual events in Cooper's books regarding how the Indian used and made bows and arrows. Cooper researched his material very carefully, and he also wrote at a time when the Indian had not been completely conquered. Some of Cooper's books are *The Pioneers*, *The Last of the Mohicans*, *The Pathfinder*, *The Deerslayer*, and *The Prairie*.

Henry Wadsworth Longfellow's famous poem, *Song of Hiawatha*, is a good example of factual material being combined with feats bordering on the legendary. Longfellow, however, gave an accurate account of how some Indians made bows and arrows. Iagoo made a bow for Hiawatha from ash. The arrows were made of oak. Flint was used for the point (fig. 4.8), and the bowstring was of dried deerskin. These materials were actually used by Indians to make archery tackle.

Longfellow described Hiawatha as being capable of breaking world records in such events as the 100- and 220-yard dashes. According to the poet, Hiawatha was so fast that he could shoot an arrow on a horizontal trajectory and outrun the arrow. That is fast even with the poor and inefficient tackle of an Indian! If any archery student can duplicate this feat, he should report to the nearest track coach immediately.

Longfellow also mentioned that Hiawatha could shoot ten arrows vertically so fast that the last arrow would be flying skyward before the first arrow had fallen. This would be virtually impossible with the tackle described in the poem.

It is recommended that the archery student look for archery references and accomplishments in literature and analyze them regarding their feasibility. The reader is referred to the following partial list as a start:

1. Aeschylus. *Agamemnon.*
2. Arnold, Elliot. *Blood Brother.*
3. Clemens, Samuel. *A Connecticut Yankee in King Arthur's Court.*
4. Defoe, Daniel. *The Adventures of Robinson Crusoe.*
5. Gillespy, Frances. *Laymon's Brut: A Comparative Study in Narrative Art.*
6. Homer. *The Illiad* and *The Odyssey.*
7. Lucian. *Dialogues of the Gods.*
8. Millar, George. *A Cross Bowman's Story.*
9. Morley, Christopher. *The Arrow.*
10. Ovid. *The Metamorphoses.*
11. Shakespeare. *Macbeth.*
12. ———. *Pericles.*
13. Stevenson, Robert Louis. *The Black Arrow.*
14. Swift, Jonathan. *Gulliver's Travels.*
15. Thucydides. *The History of The Peloponnesian War.*

ART

There are thousands of sculps and drawings involving archery in private collections, museums, and art museums throughout the world. Some of these, like the Bayeux Tapestry, are very famous, while others are obscure. Some of the earliest art forms of mankind, cave drawings, depicted bow hunters in pursuit of game. The student interested in art is invited to look for sculps and drawings involving archery.

The works of art on the following pages show various artists' concepts of archery feats, tackle, and events. The reader should study these and look for the following points: (1) the artist's concept of archery form, (2) tackle design, and (3) the artistic merit of the work.

Richard Pardons Robin Hood—
1184 A.D.—Briggs: Beale

Sennacherib (Assyria)

Cupid with bow—
Chas. Lemiore (Louvre)

Diana—Goddess of Wild Things

Courtesy of H. Armstrong Roberts. Printed by permission.

Battle of Marathon—
Briggs: Beale

Roman war elephant

Buffalo hunt with wolfskin mask—Catlin #13

Potential
benefits of archery

7

The benefits of muscular activity are many. Each sport makes unique contributions to spectators and participants. Some values may be derived covertly, but the spectator can never realize the full spectrum of values which a sport offers. To derive potential biophysical benefits, an individual must act overtly. One must become involved. The participant, unskilled or skilled, is the individual who derives the greatest benefit of sport from axiologic, psychologic, physiologic, and anatomic points of view.

Archery is usually thought of as an "easy sport" by those not cognizant of its many aspects. Granted, target practice in one's backyard or on the local archery range may not be as vigorous as a game of handball or tennis. In contrast, however, the latter two sports are not as vigorous as bow hunting for grizzly bear in the high, wilderness areas of Canada or Alaska. Archery is a sport which the participant can adjust to his own needs and physiologic status. In its many forms, archery can be engaged in by old and young, men and women, physically handicapped people and superbly conditioned athletes. Archery can be easy, but it can also be extremely difficult in many different ways. Therein lie many potential values of considerable magnitude for each archer.

The archer must utilize a large percentage of his musculature while shooting the bow. This fact is often overlooked. The shooting stance requires muscular contraction to stabilize ankles, knees, hips, pelvic girdle, and spinal column. The anteroposterior antigravity musculature (fig. 7.1) is primarily responsible for the function of keeping the archer in a stable, upright position as the bow is drawn and the arrow is released. The muscles

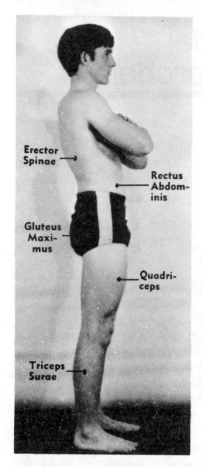

Fig. 7.1. Anteroposterior Antigravity Musculature. (From Logan and McKinney **Kinesiology**.)

which do this are the triceps surae (gastrocnemius and soleus muscles) at the ankle, quadriceps femoris muscle group at the knee, the gluteus maximus at the hip, and the erector spinae muscle group which keeps the spinal column in a vertical position. The abdominal muscles also act in an antigravity fashion. If the archer has a backward lean as he draws, the rectus abdominis muscle in particular helps pull the archer back into the proper stance position.

The antigravity muscles form a "foundation" on which skill is developed. The primary working muscles for the archer are located in the shoulder girdle, shoulder joints, elbow joints, radioulnar joints, wrists, and hands.

The major actions of the bow arm (fig. 7.2) are shoulder abduction through the lateral plane prior to the draw, elbow extension, radioulnar joint motion to a stable midposition between supination and pronation, and the wrist is extended. Fingers are extended and relaxed as much as possible. The muscles most involved for shoulder abduction are the deltoid and supraspinatus. The triceps brachii muscle keeps the elbow extended. There are five muscles most involved for the stable position exhibited by the radioulnar and wrist joints. These are the pronator teres, pronator quadratus, biceps brachii, supinator, and brachioradialis.

The major actions involving the drawing arm are elbow flexion, horizontal abduction of the shoulder joint, and scapular adduction in the shoulder girdle (figs. 7.2 and 7.3). Elbow flexion against the resistance of the bow weight is performed by the biceps brachii, brachialis, and brachioradialis muscles. Horizontal abduction of the drawing arm shoulder is performed through isotonic or shortening contraction of the deltoid, infraspinatus, teres minor, and the long head of the triceps brachii. The muscles most involved for scapular adduction are the middle fibers of the trapezius and rhomboids. The latter two muscles may be the most important

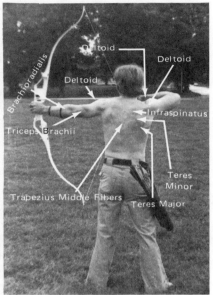

Fig. 7.2. Anterior musculature used while drawing.

Fig. 7.3. Posterior musculature used while drawing.

muscles used by the archer. As the reader can understand, there is more muscular activity involved in drawing and releasing an arrow than "meets the eye." The archer who shoots and retrieves 288 arrows during two FITA rounds has literally performed a considerable amount of physiologic work. This has many potential biophysical values for the participant.

People who work at desks have a natural tendency to let their scapulae abduct—the shoulder blades are pulled away from the spine. This lengthens muscles in the back and shortens muscles in the chest. Holding this position for prolonged periods of time causes physical discomfort. Breathing is inhibited. This adds to the tired feeling one has at the end of a working day. Shooting a bow for a period of time daily helps counteract the atypical muscular actions caused by the prolonged sitting. To draw a bow, the shoulder girdle must be pulled back by the rhomboids and trapezius muscles as the scapulae are being adducted or drawn toward the spinal column. Muscles lengthened for long periods during the day are shortened by overcoming the resistance of the bow weight. In effect, the archer is doing a highly specific type of weight training. The greatest potential benefit from this kind of activity for the desk worker is the ultimate relaxation of muscles used atypically for prolonged periods during the working day.

Contrary to popular belief, there is no evidence to support the concept that archery automatically contributes to the development of good posture. Archery does have this potential *if it is practiced extensively by young children* who have not reached anatomic and physiologic maturation.

One major criticism of our society made by sociologists and psychologists is the decline of family unity. To paraphrase a familiar theological statement: The family which plays together stays together. With the onset during the past decade of a wide variety of avocational activities for children as well as adult-centered activities for children (examples are Little League Baseball and Pop Warner Football), the family in modern America often finds itself literally and figuratively going in different directions during leisure time. Archery is one sport which can be enjoyed by all members of the family at one time at home, on a field archery range, bow hunting, bow fishing, or on a target archery range. There are psychologic and sociologic benefits inherent within an activity such as archery which has the potential to develop family unity (fig. 7.4).

Archery provides the participant with a sport which can be used throughout life. Some sport activities learned early in life do not have this potential. A man in his thirties does not engage in American football during his leisure time as an active participant. The opportunities are not available to do this, and the human body will not withstand the stresses and strain. In contrast, many excellent archers do not reach their performance peak until they are in their thirties. Archery is a sport for people of all ages.

One major biophysical value of muscular activity is the ability to release emotional tension. Emotional tension seems to be cumulative in nature. The reader has probably experienced at least one day in which everything seemed to go wrong! At the conclusion of such a day, one tends to be rather tired and tense. This type of tension is psychologic in nature. Psychiatrists indicate that it is a good idea to "blow off steam" on these occasions in a socially acceptable way. This contributes to one's mental health. Shooting the bow and arrow for an hour after a "bad day" has the potential to relax the archer. Physical work of any type has the potential to relax a human being. *The concept of work being a relaxant is so abstract that it is not too well understood by most people.*

The challenges which archery presents in its various sport forms have value for many people. Archery is not an easy sport to master, since there are many opportunities for the occurrence of human errors. This facet of archery has the greatest appeal to many sportsmen and individuals who seek perfection in things they attempt. *Mastery of archery is a motivating factor* for many archers.

The serious student of the humanities may derive enjoyment by reading and studying about the use of archery as portrayed by many authors and scholars throughout history. The mythological literature abounds with stories about archery, and art museums throughout the world contain many famous works of art depicting archers in action. The scholarly student who is interested in archery should look for these literary and artistic works as he pursues a formal education. This liberal arts approach to studying a sport is often overlooked by students and physical educators.

The individual who enjoys social activities will find that archery is a good medium for this purpose. Most cities of any size throughout the country have archery clubs which provide opportunities for the archer to share his interests with fellow archers. Clubs are locally operated by a system of self-government, and funded by modest dues. Rounds are shot periodically for practice. There are also intraclub and interclub tournaments. Members also compete in large professional and amateur tournaments conducted within the state, region, and nationally.

In contrast to the social aspect of archery, the archer who likes to be alone can practice and compete on a highly individualized basis. No partner or team is absolutely necessary to enjoy archery. It has been said that the greatest form of competition is with one's self. An archer can compete without contact with other people if he so desires.

Archery is and has been many things to many people. In contemporary society, archery is a sport for the real competitor. Archery is also for the individual who enjoys handling fine tackle; it is for the man or woman who enjoys being in the out-of-doors during a hunting season, a field archery tournament, or bow fishing; it is for the person who enjoys the spirit of competition with other people and with himself against the elements. Archery can be a partial means of making the participant's leisure time more rewarding and meaningful.

Fig. 7.4. "The Toxophilites." A pen and ink sketch by W. Murray, 1840. (From E. G. Heath, **The Grey Goose Wing.)**

The language of archery

8

Archery, like any sport or specialized area, has a vocabulary all its own, with many terms defined in a unique manner. This is necessary so archers can communicate with each other very succinctly and precisely.

The following is a partial list of terms that are used in archery commonly:

Addressing the Target. The archer's stance straddling the shooting line prior to shooting the arrow.

AMO. Archery Manufacturer's Organization.

Anchor Point. The placement of the archer's bowstring hand on the chin or face with the bow at full draw.

Archer's Paradox. The aerodynamically stabilizing condition of the arrow after it deflects around the bow handle at release.

Arm Guard. A leather protective device for the radioulnar and wrist areas of the bow arm.

Arrow Rest. A device mounted just above the arrow shelf on the bow to maintain arrow position from nocking until the arrow has cleared the bow at release.

Arrow Shelf. The lowermost area of the sight window on the bow.

Arrowsmith. An individual who specializes in making arrows and arrowheads.

Back. The side of the bow limb away from the archer when the bow is in the draw position.

Blunt. A flattened arrow point usually made of rubber or metal designed to kill small game upon impact.

Bow Arm. The arm which the archer prefers to use for holding the bow during shooting.

Bow Bracer. A device designed to insure safety for the archer during the process of bracing or stringing the bow.

Bow Hand. The hand which the archer prefers to use for holding or supporting the bow during the shooting.

Bowman. An archer.

Bowsight. An adjustable device attached to the bow which facilitates the aiming process for the archer.

Bowstrap. A leather strap which allows the archer to maintain contact with the bow without actually gripping the handle.

Bow Window. The center shot or sight window area of the bow handle immediately above the grip which aids the archer during the aiming process.

Bowyer. An individual who specializes in making bows.

Brace Height. The bow manufacturer's recommended distance from the pivot point of the bow to the bow string. Replaces the older term "fistmcle."

Bracing. The process of stringing the bow in preparation for shooting by placing the bowstring loops into position in the notches of the bow.

Broadhead. A multiple-edged and razor-sharp arrow point utilized in bow hunting.

Brush Button. A silencer, device usually rubber, placed on each end of the bowstring to reduce string noise following release during bow hunting.

Butt. The term used for target backing when the target face is mounted on a straw or hay bale.

Cant. Tilting the bow left or right by lateral or medial rotation of the shoulder joint of the bow arm.

Cast. The velocity which the bow can impart to the arrow, and the horizontal distance which the arrow can traverse.

Center Shot Bow. A bow designed to allow the arrow rest to be placed in the center of the upper limb instead of being placed at the extreme lateral side of the bow.

Clout. A type of long-distance shooting at a forty-eight-foot target drawn on the surface of the ground.

Composite Bow. A bow manufactured by utilizing two or more types of materials such as wood and fiberglass.

Creeping. An undesired forward motion of the bowstring from the anchor point immediately prior to release.

Crest. The colored identification bands on the arrow immediately inferior to the fletching.

Dead Release. Extension of the interphalangeal joints of the fingers gripping the bowstring due to the kinetic energy of the bowstring instead of to muscular force.

Draw. The process of moving the bowstring with nocked arrow from brace height to the archer's anchor point on the face.

Draw Weight. See "Weight."

Drift. The lateral displacement of an arrow from its normal trajectory due to crosswind velocity.

End. In target archery, six arrows shot consecutively.

Eye. The loop at the end of the bowstring which fits into the notch of the bow during bracing.

Face. The side of the bow limb closest to the archer when the bow is in the draw position—replaces the term "belly."

Field Captain. The man in charge of an archery tournament.

Finger Sling. A small piece of leather with loops at each end designed to fit around the archer's thumb and index or middle finger during shooting. It helps prevent the bow from falling to the ground after release.

Finger Tab. A leather device worn to prevent blistering on the anterior surface of the three drawing fingers.

FITA. Federation Internationale DeTir a L'Arc—The organization responsible for conducting world championships in archery.

Fletcher. An arrow maker.

Fletching. The stabilizing feathers or vanes attached to an arrow between the nock and crest.

Flight Shooting. An archery event in which the object is to obtain the greatest distance possible for the projected arrow.

Flinching. An undesired and sudden motion of the bow arm (usually horizontal abduction of the bow shoulder) at release.

Flu-Flu. An arrow with large or spiraled fletching designed to increase the drag coefficient in order to diminish flight distance.

Follow-through. The act of holding the release position until the arrow has struck the target.

Gap Shooting. An aiming technique whereby the archer estimates the distance (gap) between a selected point and the target. Release is made when the gap no longer exists.

Gold. The center of the target used in target archery.

Grip. The center portion of the bow where the hand exerts pressure during the draw. (This term is often used interchangeably with the term "handle.")

Grouping. The arrangement of the end of arrows on the target face after they have been shot.

Handle. The middle portion of the bow.

Handle Riser. The areas just below and above the bow grip.

Hanging Arrow. An arrow which does not penetrate the target mat, but dangles across the target face.

Hen Feathers. The two feathers on either side of the index feather. Traditionally, these feathers are not as flamboyant as the index feather.

Hit. An arrow which embeds itself within one of the scoring areas on the target face.

Holding. The act of maintaining the bow and arrow in a stable position at full draw prior to release.

Index Feather. The feather at right angle to the slit in the nock of the arrow and usually different in color from the remaining feathers. This term replaces the older term, "cock feather."

Jig. A device used for making and repairing fletching and bowstrings.

Keeper. A piece of material used to hold the bowstring to the nock when the bow is not braced.

Kiss Button. A contact point on the bowstring for the archer's lips to touch so as to insure consistency and accuracy of the anchor point.

Lady Paramount. The woman in charge of an archery tournament.

Limbs. The parts of the bow above and below the grip and riser sections.

Long Bow. A bow with no built-in curvatures to increase leverage.

Loop. The ends of the bowstring made to attach securely into the bow notches when braced.

Loose. The act of releasing or shooting the arrow.

Mass Weight. The actual or physical weight of the bow in pounds.

Mat. The firmly constructed area of the target upon which the target face is mounted.

NAA. National Archery Association of the United States.

NFAA. National Field Archery Association.

Nock. The plastic device on the end of the arrow opposite the point, made with a groove for holding the arrow to the bowstring when placed in position for shooting.

Nocking. The technique of placing the arrow on the bowstring in preparation for shooting.

Nock Locater. The stops on the serving of the bowstring which mark the exact nocking point for the arrow.

Oblique Stance. A foot position whereby the toe of the foot nearest the target is placed on a line to the target and then rotated laterally forty-five degrees. The heel of the foot farthest from the target is placed in line with the center of the target.

Open Stance. A foot position whereby the line to the target is from the instep of the foot farthest from the target while the leg nearest the target has been extended at the hip to form at least a toe-heel relationship with the foot online to the target.

Overbowed. The act of drawing a bow which has a weight out of proportion to the archer's strength.

Overdraw. Drawing the arrow beyond the face of the bow or drawing the bow to its point of maximum stress on the limbs.

Overstrung. The use of a bowstring too short for the bow which results in an excessive brace height and inefficiency in shooting.

PAA. Professional Archer's Association.

Peeking. Undesired motion of the archer's head at the time of release in an attempt to follow the arrow trajectory into the target.

Perfect End. A situation when all arrows shot are grouped tightly into the highest scoring area on the target face.

Petticoat. The outermost perimeter of the target face outside the scoring area.

Pile. A term used as a synonym for the arrow point.

Pinch. The undesired act of squeezing the arrow nock too tightly during the draw causing the arrow to move off the arrow rest.

Pivot Point. The part of the bow grip farthest from the string when the bow is braced.

Plucking. Undesired lateral motion of the string hand and arm away from the bowstring at the time of release.

Point Blank Range. The distance at which the archer may utilize the center of the target as an aiming point.

Point-of-aim. An antiquated technique of aiming whereby the archer used a mark unattached to the bow and usually placed on the ground as an alignment point.

Prism Sight. A sophisticated aiming device utilizing refraction principles to gain a clear view of the target.

Pull. The process of disengaging embedded arrows from the target.

Pushing. The undesired process of moving the bow parallel to the earth at the time of release and follow-through.

Quiver. Any device designed to hold arrows not actually being shot.

Range. (1) A specified distance to be shot during a round or while hunting; (2) an area designated for target or field archery.

Rebound. An arrow which does not penetrate the target face or mat but bounces off the target.

Recurved Bow. A bow manufactured so the ends of the limbs deflect toward the back of the bow to increase leverage when the bow is braced.

Reflexed Bow. A bow with straight limbs where the backs form an obtuse angle at the junction of the handle riser and grip.

Release. The act of putting the arrow into flight due to a release of the pressure on the bowstring by either the fingers or the release device.

Round. The term used to designate the number of arrows to be shot at specific distances at specified target faces or targets.

Scatter. Arrows distributed unevenly over a large portion of the target face and/or ground.

Scoring Area. The concentric circles on the target face worth prescribed point values.

Serving. The protective thread wrapped around the bowstring where the arrow is nocked.

Shaft. The body of the arrow upon which the nock, fletching, and point are mounted, and the crest is painted.

Shooting Glove. A three-fingered protectice device utilized by some archers for the bowstring-gripping fingers, in lieu of a finger tab.

Shooting Line. The line straddled by archers during shooting which indicates a specific distance from the target in target archery.

Sight Window. The area of the bow cut away to allow the arrow rest to be mounted in the center of the bow.

Snake. Embedding of an arrow under grass and horizontal to the ground, making the arrow extremely difficult to locate.

Spine. The measured deflection in inches of an arrow shaft when it is depressed by a two-pound weight at its center.

Stabilizer. A weighted device added to the handle-riser area of the bow designed to reduce torque and absorb shock upon release.

Stacking. A disproportionate increase in bow weight during the last few inches of the draw.

String Fingers. The fingers used to hold the nocked arrow in place on the bowstring.

String Height. See "Brace height."

String Notch. The grooves at the distal ends of the bow limbs, designed to hold the bowstring when the bow is braced.

Tackle. All equipment used by an archer.

Target Captain. The individual at each target designated to determine and call the score of each arrow and pull each arrow from the target.

Target Face. The scoring area of a target.

Target Mat. The backing of the target which the arrows penetrate.

Tassel. A piece of material used to clean arrows.

Timber. A verbal warning given in field archery that an arrow is being released.

Tip. The ends of the bow limbs.

Torque. An undesirable twisting of the bow and/or bowstring during any part of the shooting process.

Toxopholite. An individual interested in archery as a performer and/or from an academic point of view.

Trajectory. The parabolic flight pattern of an arrow following release.

Underbowed. The act of drawing a bow with a weight too light to enable the archer to accomplish the shooting objective.

Understrung. A bow with a bowstring too long which results in an improper brace height and reduced efficiency.

Vane. A term used most commonly when fletching is made of plastic or rubber instead of feathers.

Wand. A historic type of target; a piece of balsa wood two inches in width embedded in the ground and projecting six feet upward from it.

Weight. The bow manufacturer's determined number of pounds required to draw each bow's string a given distance.

Wrist Sling. A device which fits around the bow and the archer's wrists designed to prevent the bow from falling to the ground as the arrow is released.

Yaw. Unstable action of the arrow during its trajectory.

Selected bibliography

Archery Magazine. P.O. Box H, Palm Springs, Calif.

Archery World. Archery Associates, Inc. Box 124, Boyerstown, Pa.

Ascham, Roger. *Toxophilus.* London: A. Murray and Son, 1545.

Barrett, Jean A. *Archery.* Pacific Palisades, Calif: Goodyear Publishing Co., 1969.

Bow and Arrow Magazine. 550-A South Citrus Avenue, Covina, Calif.

- Burke, Edmund H. *Archery Handbook.* New York: Arco Publishing Co., Inc., 1965.

———. *The History of Archery.* New York: William Morrow & Co., 1957. 1957.

Butler, David F. *The New Archery.* New York: A. S. Barnes & Co., 1968.

Campbell, Donald W. *Archery.* Englewood Cliffs, N. J.: Prentice-Hall, Inc., 1971.

Driscoll, Margaret L., ed. *Selected Archery Articles.* Washington, D.C.: American Association for Health, Physical Education, and Recreation, 1971.

Elmer, Robert P. *American Archery.* Ronks, Pa.: National Archery Association of the United States, 1917.

Elmer, Robert P., and Faris, Nabih A. *Arab Archery.* Princeton, N. J.: Princeton University Press, 1945.

Elmer, Robert P. *Archery.* Philadelphia: Penn Publishing Co., 1926.

Ford, Horace A., *Archery: Its Theory and Practice.* London: J. Buchanan, 1856.

Gannon, Robert. *The Complete Book of Archery.* New York: Coward-McCann, Inc., 1964.

Gillelan, G. Howard. *Complete Book of the Bow and Arrow.* Harrisburg, Pa.: The Stackpole Co., 1971.

Grogan, Hiram J. *Modern Bow Hunting.* Harrisburg, Pa.: The Stackpole Co., 1958.

Haugen, Arnold O., and Metcalf, Harlan. *Field Archery and Bowhunting.* New York: Ronald Press Co., 1963.

Heath, E. G., ed. *Anecdotes of Archery*. London: The Tabard Press Ltd., 1970.

Heath, E. G. *The Grey Goose Wing*. Reading, Berkshire, England: Osprey Publishing Ltd., 1971.

Herrigel, Eugen. *Zen in the Art of Archery*. New York: Pantheon Books, 1953.

Herter, George L., and Hofmeister, Russell. *Professional & Amateur Archery Tournament and Hunting Instructions and Encyclopedia*. Waseca, Minn.: Herter's Inc., 1963.

Hickman, C. N.; Nagler, F.; and Klopsteg, Paul E. *Archery: The Technical Side*. Redlands, Calif.: National Field Archery Assoc. of the U. S., 1947.

Hill, Howard. *Hunting the Hard Way*. Chicago: Follett Publishing Co., 1953.

Hougham, Paul C. *The Encyclopedia of Archery*. New York: A. S. Barnes & Co., 1957.

Keaggy, Dave. *Power Archery*. Drayton Plains, Mich.: Power Archery Products, 1968.

Klann, Margaret L. *Target Archery*. Reading, Pa.: Addison-Wesley Publishing Co., 1970.

Klopsteg, P. E. "Physics of Bows and Arrows." *American Journal of Physics* 11(August, 1943):175-92.

Logan, Gene A., and McKinney, Wayne C. *Kinesiology*. Dubuque, Ia.: Wm. C. Brown Company Publishers, 1970.

Longman, C. J., and Walrond, H. *Archery*. New York: Frederick Ungar Publishing Co., 1894.

Love, Albert J. *Field Archery Technique*. Corpus Christi, Tex.: Dotson Printing Co., 1956.

Markham, Gervase. *The Art of Archerie*. London: Arms and Armour Press, 1968.

Niemeyer, Roy K. *Beginning Archery*. Belmont, Calif.: Wadsworth Publishing Co., Inc., 1967.

Pope, Saxton. *Yahi Archery*. Berkeley: University of California Press, 1918.

———. *Hunting with Bow and Arrow*. New York: G. P. Putnam's Sons, 1947.

———. *The Adventurous Bowman*. New York: G. P. Putnam's Sons, 1926.

Pszczola, Lorraine. *Archery*. Philadelphia: W. B. Saunders Co., 1971.

Rhode, Robert J. *Archery Champions*. Norristown, Pa.: The Archers' Publishing Co., 1961.

Schuyler, Keith C. *Archery: From Golds to Big Game*. New York: A. S. Barnes & Co., 1970.

Sterling, Sara. *Robin Hood and His Merry Men*. Philadelphia: George W. Jacobs and Co., 1921.

Thompson, Maurice and Thompson, Will H. *How to Train in Archery*. New York: E. I. Horsman, 1879.

Thompson, Maurice. *The Witchery of Archery*. New York: Charles Scribner's Sons, 1878.

Wilson, R. I., ed. *Basic Instruction for Classes*. Hickory Corners, Mich.: Professional Archers Association, 1964.

Appendix:
Questions and answers

1. Which one of the following battles marked the decline of archery as a formidable war weapon?
   a. Battle of Agincourt   C. Battle of Spanish Armada
   b. Battle of New Orleans   d. Battle of Hastings   (p. 78)
2. Which one of the following is not a part of a bow?
   a. nock   b. sight window   c. limb   D. Shaft   (p. 9)
3. Recommended bow weight for women target archers is:
   a. 10-14 pounds   b. 15-19 pounds   C. 20-30 pounds   d. 35-45 pounds (p. 11)
4. For accuracy, the best arrows are made of:
   A. aluminum   c. Port Orford cedar
   b. fiberglass   d. pine   (p. 2)
5. The part of the arrow that acts as a stabilizer in flight is the:
   A. fletching   b. crest   c. pile   d. shaft   (p. 5)
6. The most important part of archery tackle is the:
   a. arm guard   b. finger tab   c. recurve bow   D. arrow   (p. 2)
7. The term "spine" may be defined as:
   a. the lateral deviations of an arrow in flight
   b. the medial deviations of an arrow shaft
   C. the stiffness of the arrow shaft
   d. the stiffness of the arrow shaftment   (p. 3)
8. The most commonly used quiver by target archers is the:
   a. shoulder quiver   c. bow quiver
   B. hip quiver   d. ground quiver   (p. 17)
9. The often stance for the right-handed archer should be with the:
   a. left foot farther from the target than the right foot
   B. left foot moved backwards slightly after assuming an even stance
   c. weight distributed on the heels
   d. majority of the weight distributed on the right foot   (p. 25)
10. The pressure of the bow hold should be felt most at the:
    a. wrist
    b. thumb
    C. thumb-index finger junction
    d. distal ends of the thumb and four fingers   (p. 28)
11. If vertical fluctuations are noted in the arrow flight pattern, the nocking angle can be adjusted by:
    A. moving the nocking point upward on the bowstring
    b. moving the nocking point downward on the bowstring

    c. rotating the arrow on its longitudinal axis

    d. changing the angles of fletching placement on the shaft   (p. 27)

12. The term "drawing" may be defined as the act of pulling:
    a. an arrow from the target
    b. an arrow from a quiver
    C. the bowstring to the anchor point.
    d. the bowstring to the medial aspect of the zygomatic arch   (p. 29)

13. An archer "follows-through" when he:
    A. holds his form until the arrow is in the target
    b. turns his shoulders toward the target after releasing the arrow
    c. steps toward the target as the arrow is released
    d. pulls his bow arm to the left while releasing the arrow   (p. 38)

14. Which one of the following bracing methods is recommended for safety and efficiency?
    a. push-pull   b. step-through   c. bow sling   D. bowstringer   (p. 21)

15. A round in target archery consists of:
    a. three arrows   c. both a. and b.
    b. six arrows   D. none of the above   (p. 45)

16. An archer is shooting her last end of arrows in a Columbia Round. She has three in the gold, one in the blue, one in the white, and one arrow passes through the target. Her score would be:
    a. 38   B. 40   c. 42   d. 44   (p. 38)

17. An archer is shooting his last end of arrows in an American Round. He has two in gold, two hit the gold and bounce off, one hits the white and bounces off, and one goes through the target. His score would be:
    A. 46   b. 44   c. 42   d. 40   (p. 38)

18. If an arrow bisects the line between the red and gold on a target archery face, but does not break the gold, the score is:
    a. 3   b. 5   c. 7   D. 9   (p. 38)

19. If you were making a clout target, what would the diameter of the outermost ring measure?
    a. 48 inches   b. 48 centimeters   c. 48 meters   D. 48 feet   (p. 47)

20. The pivot point of a bow is where the
    a. bow string is attached to the bow   c. stabilizer fits on the bow
    B. bow hold is made   d. arrow rest is placed   (p. 28)

21. The term "bracing a bow" implies that an archer is:
    a. leaning on a bow   c. backing a bow
    B. stringing a bow   d. kissing a bow   (p. 21)

22. A blunt arrow point would be appropriate for hunting which one of the following animals?
    A. rabbit   b. deer   c. bobcat   d. coyote   (p. 59)

23. The term "brace height" is defined as:
    a. the grip area of the bow
    b. the distance between the fingers and the arrow nock
    c. the distance between the finger and the bow nocks
    D. the distance between the bow handle and the string   (p. 23)

24. The term "serving" is defined as:
    a. the colored portion of the arrow inferior to the fletching
    b. the eye or loop of the bowstring
    C. the string wrapping at the middle of the bowstring
    d. the act of releasing the arrow toward the target   (p. 15)

25. Johann von Schiller wrote about a dramatic arrow shot in his story of:
    a. *The Black Arrow*   C. *Wilhelm Tell*
    b. *A Cross Bowman's Story*   d. *Adventures of Robin Hood*   (p. 83)

26. The first English textbook on archery was written by a noted Englishman:
    a. L. Dennis Humphrey   c. Mike McKinney
    b. Gene A. Logan   D. Roger Ascham   (p. 78)

27. Undue pressure exerted by the index finger on the arrow nock at the time of release will cause:

A. vertical fluctuations in the flight of the arrow
b. horizontal fluctuations in the flight of the arrow
c. the arrow to go over the target when shooting from 40 yards
d. muscle cramps within the archer's "arrow hand"   (p. 30)

28. The most important part of the release is:
    a. finger extension of the "bow hand"
    b. finger extension of the "arrow hand"
    c. arm extension of the "bow arm"
    D. relaxation of the "arrow hand"   (p. 37)

29. The term "centershot" is defined as:
    a. a worn target face
    b. an archer who shoots in the middle of a group of archers
    c. a hit in the center of the gold on a target archery face
    D. a bow that has been cut to its center axis above the Pint Point (p. 10)

30. For a right-handed archer, it is known that an arrow leaves the bow from
    five to seven degrees to the:
    a. right   c. rear of the arrow rest (belly)
    B. left   d. front of the arrow rest (back) (p. 4)

31. An archer who has a twenty-eight inch draw is recommended to use a bow
    length of:
    a. 60 inches   b. 62 inches   C. 64 inches   d. 66 inches   (p. 13)

32. The most functional bow manufactured is the:
    a. long bow   B. takedown bow   c. duoflexed bow   d. composite bow (p. 10)

COMPLETION

33. Archaeologists believe that man first used the bow and arrow during the
    (upper Paleolithic) period.   (p. 70)

34. (Ghenghis Khan) was one of the first war leaders to mobilize his archers by
    putting them on horseback.   (p. 73)

35. King Henry V led his archers into battle against the French in 1414 A.D.
    This battle took place at (Agincourt).   (p. 75)

36. In mythology, the term "Sagittarius" means (archer).   (p. 79)

37. In Greek mythology, (Apollo) was the God of Archery.   (p. 80)

38. The potential, maximum score for the American Round is (810) points. (p. 46)

39. The official publication of the National Field Archery Association is
    (Archery Magazine).   (p. 44)

40. The fact that an arrow deviates to the left for a right-handed archer as it
    leaves the bow but travels directly to the target is known as the (archer's
    paradox).   (p. 4)

41. Historical segments of archers at the Battle of Hastings were depicted on
    the (Bayeux tapestry).   (p. 71)

42. The (antero posterior antigravity) muscles help the archer maintain a stable,
    vertical shooting position.   (p. 88)

43. A bow is usually marked for its weight at a (twenty-eight inch) draw. (p. 10)

44. The portion of the bow immediately below the arrow rest is known as the
    (arrow shelf).   (p. 18)

45. Gripping the bow is a mistake, because this will cause (fatigue) of forearm
    musculature.   (p. 28)

46. Most large game animals are killed with the bow and arrow by the (hemor-
    rhage) technique.   (p. 59)

47. Brush buttons are attached to the bowstring to serve as (string silencers). (p. 56)

48. The (index) feather is usually placed in an outward position from the bow. (p. 26)

49. The organization which controls archery throughout the world is (Federa-
    tion Internationale De Tir A L'Arc).   (p. 44)

50. A field archery course consists of fourteen targets known collectively as a
    (unit).   (p. 48)

Index